PRAISE FOR
THE THIRD CIRCLE

"*The Third Circle Protocol* speaks the truth. One plus one equals three. The third entity is the relationship which two people create. My wife calls marriage a struggle and Joseph Campbell called it an ordeal because they understand the effort that goes into creating the third circle. The Third Circle can show you the way to create a healthy relationship and be your life coach."

— *BERNIE SIEGEL, MD*, author of *The Art of Healing* and *365 Prescriptions for the Soul*

"*The Third Circle Protocol* serves as a clear portal for those who live in their heads to move beyond an abstract idea of enriching relationships. This book provides specific and practical steps that one may take to establish a 'relationship blueprint' that aligns ones values and priorities with actions. It covers a wide range of relationship types and scenarios to help one recognize needs, to achieve goals and to realize one's vision of success in relationships. The protocol is concrete and powerful and, when applied, it works."

— *MARY SUSAN MACDONALD*, Board Director, Mensa Canada

"Anyone who's in a couple, has parent-child tensions, an over-critical friend or a difficult boss, can benefit from reading *The Third Circle Protocol*. Its basic principles—have a healthy understanding of your own values and priorities, then consider the relationship with another as a separate entity—are now made understandable and practical to apply through this book. All relationships are complex, and most people give lip service to 'working on it,' but get lost in their own separateness. Georgina Cannon provides a map and exercises to get you and your relationships to a better place. She posits the relationship as a contract to be 'nourished, nurtured, respected and heard'... It's not always easy but, with practice, becomes a more promising route to relationship satisfaction and success."

— *ELLIE TESHER*, syndicated advice columnist, "Ellie" *www.ellieadvice.com*

"In *The Third Circle Protocol*, Cannon illustrates the importance of appreciating that a relationship between two people is a living growing entity, requiring nourishment and care. She provides inspiration to create vital relationships not only by knowing our values, priorities and needs but what we have to contribute. By following her rich and practical guidelines, we are positioned well to co-create fulfilling romantic partnerships as well as other rewarding friendships."

— *LINDA BLOOM*, co-author of *101 Things I Wish I Knew When I Got Married, Secrets of Great Marriages* and *Happily Ever After... and Thirty-nine Other Myths About Love.*

D1057779

THE THIRD
CIRCLE PROTOCOL

How to relate to yourself and others
in a healthy vibrant, evolving way,
Always and All-Ways

Georgina Cannon, Msc.D

FINDHORN PRESS

Published in 2016 by Findhorn Press, Scotland

ISBN 978-1-84409-710-4

Edited by Nicky Leach
Cover design by Richard Crookes
Interior design by Damian Keenan
Printed and bound in the USA

DISCLAIMER
The information in this book is given in good faith and is neither
intended to diagnose any physical or mental condition nor to serve
as a substitute for informed medical advice or care.
Please contact your health professional for medical advice and
treatment. Neither author nor publisher can be held liable by any
person for any loss or damage whatsoever which may arise from the
use of this book or any of the information therein.

Published by
Findhorn Press
117-121 High Street,
Forres IV36 1AB,
Scotland, UK

t +44 (0)1309 690582
f +44 (0)131 777 2711
e info@findhornpress.com
www.findhornpress.com

Contents

Live not for battles won, for the-end-of-the-song.
Live in the along.

PULITZER PRIZE–WINNING POET

Acknowledgments

To everyone who is part of the tapestry of my life, the warp and weft of those that bring light, and those who brought the shade. Those in business, those in pleasure. Clients in the clinic. Students in my classes. Those who passed through briefly, those who stay, and stayed, along for the bumpy ride, I am blessed. I am grateful beyond measure. Without relationships and connections we are hollow. Without the love, support, kindness, and recognition that we echo off each other, we are soundless.

There are a few I need to mention: Debbi Lockie, my manager, who keeps my feet firmly planted on the ground yet understands my need to fly; Penny Hozy, the best editor ever; my agent, Devra Jacobs, for her gentle but firm guiding hand with all my books; and my beloved long-time loving, caring, patient Canadian friends, plus my family in Israel, who are there always. Blessed be.

The purpose of all relationships is to create a sacred context within which you can express the fullness of who you are.

— NEALE DONALD WALSCH,
CONVERSATIONS WITH GOD

Introduction —
About the Third Circle

It was the bookkeeper who started it all. Robert, my client, had recently inherited his family business, and that included the long-time loyal bookkeeper along with other employees.

"She's been with us for over 25 years, and she still treats me like I was eight years old!" he complained. "She still calls me Bobby-boy."

Robert had been endeavoring to install new systems and services into his lighting design company and was meeting with resistance from the bookkeeper at every turn.

"Helen is a sweetheart, and she carries the company history with her," he explained, "which is good and bad news! She hates change and laughs every time I bring the staff together to discuss a new design process or ordering and invoicing system. It doesn't matter what it is, she keeps reminding me that if it's not broken, don't fix it. And she brings cookies for me. I don't want her damn cookies!" At that moment he looked—and sounded—like an eight-year-old boy!

As I started working with Robert on both his snapshot version of himself and his snapshot version of Helen over the first few weeks, the idea for this new protocol was born; a protocol that allowed new rules and boundaries for their new relationship. Robert and Helen were in a relationship, whether they liked it or not. A relationship exists between any two people who work together, live together, play golf together, or engage in a simple transaction, such as buying and providing coffee and donuts.

The new protocol involves examining expectations, unwritten or unsaid mind contracts, assumptions, previous patterns of bullying or victimhood—

whatever ends in disruption, discomfort, and discord. Some of these are learned behaviors from childhood, some from previous lifetime patterns, and some from careless ignorance of what it takes to have a healthy relationship. However, we know, at our deepest level, that the relationships we create are absolutely critical to our success as a human being on this planet at this time.

Hence the need for a new process or protocol. Over the following couple of years, this protocol was refined and developed by working with different levels of relationships: a teenage daughter with her mother; friends who had drifted apart but still loved each other; a middle-aged daughter and her father who was showing signs of dementia; lots of married or living-together couples—both straight and gay; a teenage boy who felt like an outsider at school, where I used the protocol to develop the relationship with himself.

Sometimes, I was fortunate enough to work with both sides of the relationship; other times, I could work with just one person, who then took the worksheets, ideas, and behaviors into their relationship and endeavored to make it work that way. Sometimes it did; sometimes it didn't. At the very least, the client had a clearer idea of what they wanted and could give—and get—from their relationships.

Since developing this protocol, I have used it myself, both in the office at the clinic and in my relationships with my family, clients, students, lovers, colleagues, and friends. It works brilliantly every time there's a misunderstanding or miscommunication. In the beginning, I used it as I needed it; today, I use it with every new client to help define their relationship with themselves before we move on to other issues and other relationships. I also use it personally at the start of every relationship, making sure we're both on the same page and have a common understanding of what this relationship is and how it will unfold with a vision of the final relationship circle.

The Relationship Circle

What is the relationship circle? Ah, so glad you asked! Now we can begin the book.

In the "olden days," we thought that relationships worked best this way. Both for husband and wife and employees and employers. Both married couples and employees/employers thought their role was to be cared for by their husband or employer.

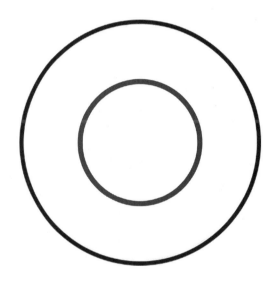

We then became more "enlightened" and realized that to some extent we are responsible for ourselves, but we still want to be partnered up or connected at differing levels with each other. So we devised a relationship that looks something like this:

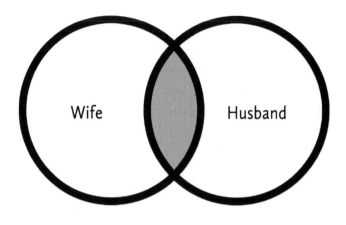

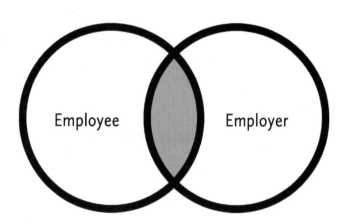

But that still doesn't work because we are still not responsible for ourselves and the outcome of our behavior, hard work, attitude, or results. That's when I developed the protocol of the Third Circle, where the relationship becomes a separate entity on its own, to be nurtured and respected. No longer do the discussions, arguments, or irrational feelings go through the "she said, he said." Now, every word, action, thought, and behavior moves towards keeping the relationship healthy, evolving, and fruitful.

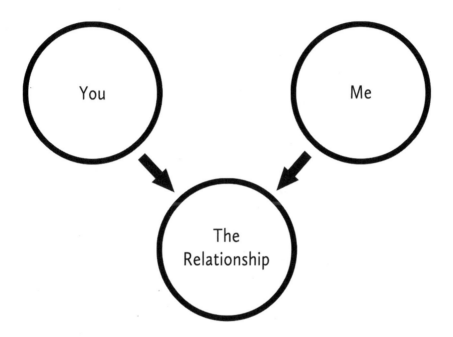

Because the focus is outside of the personalities involved, there is a stronger chance of a successful responsible relationship. Between teens and parents. Siblings. Employees and employers. Lovers and friends. This protocol gives space and direction for more opportunities of success by writing the heretofore unwritten relationship contract.

Assumptions are the termites of relationships.

— HENRY WINKLER

CHAPTER 1

The Third Circle Protocol

The meeting of two personalities is like the contact of two chemical substances; if there is any reaction, both are transformed.

— CARL JUNG

RELATIONSHIP = the emotional or other connection between people: a connection, association, or involvement

The genesis of the word relationship is two-fold, from both the German words *gemeinschaft* (social relationship based on affection or kinship) and *Gesellschaft* (social relationship based on duty to society or an organization). Which pretty well sums it up … except that things are always more than they seem.

For more years than I would care to admit to, I have worked in relationships with clients—in the corporate world as a journalist, a senior public relations/marketing executive, as a business coach and as a clinical hypnotist and counselor. In all cases, relationships are key. For most of us, each day consists of moving from one relationship to another, from the time we wake up in the morning until the time we ease into sleep at night. And most of us give very little thought to these relationships, except briefly maybe, at the start of romantic relationships, which can occupy our thoughts and body reactions way too much at the beginning of the relationship only to curiously peter out within a short time. (*I wonder what I did? I wonder what happened?*)

I believe that we spend more time choosing a flavor of ice cream to eat than we give thought to how we start, build, and live in our relationships. And that includes the relationship we have with ourselves—because we take ourselves everywhere we go! And that can be a real problem if you don't have a relationship with yourself to know what you offer and what you want in a relationship. And that means *all* relationships: at home, in business, with friends, with family. Until now, there has been no way to plan and live in mutually satisfying relationships, except with luck, and we all know how tenuous luck can be!

> *We were always meant to work in partnership — we of nature and man. The very physical existence of man on Earth has depended upon all kingdoms of nature... Man and nature, come together as we have on this planet, hold the promise and potential many times their individual power...*
>
> — MACHEALLE SMALL WRIGHT,
> *FOUNDER OF PERELANDRA*

Over the years, working with thousands of clients, I came to realize that we are always in a relationship of some sort, usually with another person, but not always. We have a relationship with ourselves, of course, that is always there. You can't hide from yourself—at least, not for long; something always catches up with you. It could be memories of better or worse times, or guilt, or pride in accomplishment, disappointment, sorrow, illness, or recovery.

When you come home at night after a hard day, you always speak to someone. You may ask yourself what you want for dinner. Or chat with your partner or kids. Or you may speak to your dog or cat as you open their can of food. Even the goldfish gets a word or two as you sprinkle food in its bowl. The plants need water. (Okay, maybe I'm getting carried away.) But as I observed and thought about all these relationships, both simple and complex, I began to see that a relationship contains three components: you, someone or something else, and the actual coming together of the two of you: the relationship itself, the Third Circle.

In brief, the Third Circle Protocol is about the unspoken expectations and agreements that we have with each other. Each person involved in a relationship of any kind is focused on their own circle of reality. The Third Circle takes the relationship out of the realm of he and she, employee and employer, teenager and parent, doctor and patient, and makes it a separate entity, with its own wants and needs.

> *As we interact with others, we read messages about who we are*
> *for them and we send messages about who we expect, want, and*
> *need them to be for us.*
>
> — RUTHELLEN JOSSELSON, JASON ARONSON

Then I began to think about the components of each of these separate entities and how they were different or similar in each of these relationships. For example, do our expectations of a husband or wife have anything in common with our expectations of our doctor or therapist? Yes, possibly.

For example, how can I confide in my therapist if I think he doesn't respect me or understand me? How can I put my life in my doctor's hands if I don't trust her? Do I expect my boss to love me the way my husband does? Of course not. Do I expect my husband to know why I have a pain in my side? Maybe, if he's a doctor. But probably not. How much loyalty do I expect from each of these relationship partners? Maybe, I thought, I could assign a number value to differentiate between them. And that's how the Third Circle Protocol started to take shape.

The Third Circle Protocol: Basic Premise And Real Life

A few years ago, I was chatting with my sister about our relationship. Over numerous cups of tea and, if I remember correctly, moving into a couple of glasses of wine, we talked about our feelings, both good and bad, our suppositions, and what we thought the other was thinking of the many years we've spent together and apart. For two people who came from the same parents and lived in the same environment, we really do see the world very differently. But we both were operating from a snapshot of that person from each of our points of view that we had taken when younger—and that snapshot was confirmed every time something did or didn't happen the way we expected it to. Sound familiar?

This often happens with children as they become adults. We have the snapshot of them and don't understand why they don't respond well to suggestions of what to eat, how to behave, or which choice to make. Married couples experience the snapshot paradigm all the time. "She's not the woman I married," says the husband 15 years into the relationship. "He's changed," a client complains about her husband who has discovered golf.

"Of course they've changed; we all do," I explain. "If we didn't, we'd still all be wearing diapers and crawling on the floor." Nature evolves. We all learn and change, even minutely, at a cellular level, every minute of every day. Emotions shift. Illness takes its toll. Finances, family, and friends all impact us. How is it possible NOT to change?

> *Who we are to the other is not identical with who we are to ourselves—and who others are to us is not who they are to themselves—or, for that matter, to other people.*
> — RUTHELLEN JOSSELSON, JASON ARONSON

We expect those around us to take us just the way we are. Right? So how come we can't do the same—take the people around us just the way they are?

In whichever relationship we're examining, we have to account for and accept the existence of change. Unfortunately (or fortunately!), things never stay the same. So maybe we have to reexamine our relationships from time to time—maybe as often as once or twice a year—to make sure we haven't lost track of our agreed-to vision. It's possible to get sidetracked for years if we're not paying attention. Haven't you ever said, "When things get back to normal…?" But what's normal? The way we felt yesterday? The way our children behaved five years ago? "Normal" is a moving target, hard to pin down. Normal is what we expect, but is it what we have?

Inside each of us is a unique person resulting from millennia of environment and heredity combined in a way that could never happen again and never ever have happened before. We aren't blank slates, but we are also communal creatures who are born before our brains are fully developed, so we're very sensitive to our environment.

— GLORIA STEINEM

Expectations, unwritten or unsaid mind contracts, assumptions, previous patterns of bullying or victimhood—whatever you want to call it, ends in disruption, discomfort, and discord. Some of these are learned behaviors from childhood, some from previous lifetime patterns, and some from careless ignorance of what it takes to have a healthy relationship. However, we know at our deepest level that the relationships we create are absolutely critical to our success as a human being on this planet at this time.

The Third Circle Protocol solves the relationship problem by treating the relationship as a separate entity—a contract, to be nourished, nurtured, respected, and heard, separate from the I/me ego.

With the Third Circle Protocol, we look at the unwritten contracts made; the wants, needs, values, and priorities within the desired relationship; plus what each partner is prepared to give to care for the relationship as a separate entity. And we write them down so that we can go back and review them and revise them, if necessary. We then compare our wants, needs, values, and priorities with those of our partner to see whether we're on the same page, to see how close or how far apart we are from each other, and whether we can bridge the gap between us and create and maintain a strong, healthy relationship. Or whether, perhaps, we're not meant for each other.

In the case of having a healthy relationship with oneself, the same rules apply, and if you think that it's simpler dealing with just one person—you—rather than a couple, you'll be surprised. Most often it's harder. We have no one to blame or focus on except ourselves.

One of the first things we do is examine and list our key values. And that means thinking about them in a way we maybe haven't before. We may value the BMW we paid so much money for, but that's not going to get us through a crisis or save our marriage. Do we put our relationship ahead of the car? Ahead of the job? The kids? Do we value peace and quiet ahead of the kids? Because if we do, we need to think very hard about how we're going to get that peace and quiet and still raise our kids in a responsible way. I think you see where this is going.

Next we examine our priorities, from a list of 15, including love, family, friendship, and fame. Knowing our priorities helps us set goals, short and long term. And when we re-examine our priorities, we discover whether they're still as important to us as they were a year ago or whether they've changed—which they often do.

Knowing our values and our priorities helps us negotiate our relationships. It's how we learn to set boundaries, once we've learned what matters to us and also to our partner in the relationship: husband, kids, therapist, boss, colleagues, and all the rest. You can't be bullied if you play to your strengths not your weaknesses. You can handle setbacks better if you know what matters most in the situation.

> *The road from intending to having is built on choosing. Over and over and over, step by step.*
>
> — JULIA B. COLWELL

Think of relationships gone wrong and ask yourself if they could have succeeded with better knowledge and understanding of each other. Could the Third Circle have been stronger if the protocol had been used to build it? Relationships can appear to be working on some levels but end up imploding because they're not working on others. You could be making tons of money at your job, but you're always at loggerheads with your boss and, if you admit it, you hate the company and its values; they're incompatible with your own key values. The sex with your wife or husband or lover might be terrific, the best ever, but you never talk to each other. She hates football, you hate restaurants; she thinks your mother is always interfering and you drink too much. You think she's a nag and her mother doesn't care enough about your kids. Is this a recipe for a good relationship?

But maybe if you'd gone through the stages of the Third Circle Protocol, you could have saved yourself (and your partner) a lot of grief and either not embarked on a relationship, or set out to fix the things that could potentially go wrong between you.

Most of us are familiar with GPS systems, either hand held or in the car, and the voice that comes with it ("Re-calculating, re-calculating") when we make a wrong turn. Why not apply the functions of global positioning devices when rethinking our relationships?

According to Wikipedia, GPS devices are able to indicate:

- the roads or paths available
- traffic congestion and alternative routes
- roads or paths that might be taken to get to the destination
- if some roads are busy (now or historically) the best route to take
- the location of food, banks, hotels, fuel, airports, or other places of interests
- the shortest route between the two locations, and
- the different options to drive on highway or back roads.

Maybe for you, the idea of "re-calculating," as you do when driving or finding your way around a new area, might be more fun and less self-judgmental as you make changes along the route of life's relationships.

With that thought in mind, the relationship possibilities are endless! Here we go. We're re-calculating our relationships. All of them!

But first, before plunging into the Third Circle with someone else, you need to figure out who *you* are and work on the relationship with yourself. Once you embark on that journey, you'll be amazed at how confident you'll begin to feel in your ability to successfully engage in relationships with others. And they, in turn, will participate in setting mutually satisfying, realistic goals for the relationship they have with you.

One way to begin the process (and we will do this with every relationship we discuss) and keep to the goal of a successful relationship is to ask yourself the following questions:

- How do I keep this relationship healthy?
- What did I do today that seemed to improve the relationship?
- Did my actions enhance and enrich the relationship for the long term?
- What are my concerns today about this relationship?
- Is there something I need to do right away to correct it?
- If not right away, when?
- What do I really *want* from this relationship?

CHAPTER 2

To Begin —
You + You: Your Relationship with Yourself

They always say time changes things, but you actually have to change them yourself.

— ANDY WARHOL

> The word circus comes from the Greek kirkos, meaning circle or ring. In the circus we call life, who's the ringmaster? The lion tamer? The daredevil high-wire artist? The clown? What is your audience hoping for? What role are you playing?

For the past 20+ years, I have worked with thousands of corporate and other clients in a clinical setting and have successfully developed the Third Circle Protocol. Ultimately, every relationship comes down to the relationship we have with ourselves. Do we treat ourselves with respect? Are we honest with ourselves? Do we listen and take notice of what our mind, body, and spirit need from us? Do we treat ourselves as we would a good and kind friend? This is not about being self-centered or ego-driven; it's about building the foundation for effective, contributing relationships—with another person, a group, and a community.

Let's take a closer look at this. It's not unusual to see people around us put themselves last. Mother, business mogul, or metaphysical counselor, male or female—no matter who they are, for many people, everyone and everything else comes first. Work, children, the endless list of must-dos and appointments, meetings, social obligations, the self—our self—gets lost in the dust and noise of every day. Add to that the list of emotions we may carry from childhood, adulthood, and sometimes society, such as anger, jealousy, low self-esteem, guilt, sadness, and fear, can add a toxic screen to how we see and interact in our world.

> *We are always getting ready to live but never living.*
>
> — RALPH WALDO EMERSON

On top of all that are the stories we believe that others have told us about ourselves and we have told ourselves about ourselves. It's a bit like being a fish in a bowl of water. The fish only knows it's in water when you take it out; otherwise it's the norm. When you live in your own fishbowl, believing what you believe, acting the way you've always acted and reacted, without awareness, you end up staying inside the fishbowl, always looking out at the world, instead of growing, learning, and experiencing life on the outside.

> *At their heart, all relationships are spiritual experiences. They nurture us, teach us and connect us to the soul of others, and most significantly, to the depth of our very own souls. Through the growth of these various relationships, and our continued journey on the path of emotional freedom, we discover extended states of awareness, which stretch out from our soul.*
>
> — DEEPAK CHOPRA,
> *ON THE WEBSITE NATURAL AWAKENINGS*

One of the ways to have a real relationship with yourself and others is to know who you truly are—the good, the bad, and the ugly. And, of course, it's all good, because you can choose. You're in charge. Or are you?

Let's find out.

Your Values

Without a strong relationship and understanding of self, it's virtually impossible to have a strong and deeply lasting relationship with others, or any sort of relationship. We have to know who we are before we know what we want/need/can offer in a relationship with another person.

List your key six or eight Life Values. Be honest; no point in pretending here. Maybe you have only four or six key values. List them in any order.

1. _____

2. _____

3. _____

4. _____

5. _____

6. _____

7. _____

8. _____

Your values are the bedrock on which you stand. They set your boundaries. Realistically speaking, how can you have a relationship with anyone else if you don't know who you are? If you live your life according to your values, other people know where you stand and who you are.

Once you look over the values chart again, ask yourself—and be honest here—do you live your values? For instance, if one of your values is honesty, are you always honest with yourself? If you value kindness, are you kind to yourself?

If there's more than two no's in the list, it's likely that your boundaries are weak. Folks walk all over you, and you complain that you're always being taken advantage of. Consider what you might do to change that.

*You create your own experience by and through the choices
you make every day. This choice-making creates your own
experience, because with every choice you make comes a certain
consequence.*

— PHILLIP C. MCGRAW ("DR. PHIL")

Your Priorities

Rank in order of importance to you and change the wording in each category
if you wish.

☐ **ACHIEVEMENT** to accomplish a major goal in life, to reach a peak
event or performance

☐ **AFFLUENCE** to amass quantities of money or property

☐ **AUTHORITY** to possess the position and power to control persons
and events

☐ **ENJOYMENT** to lead a happy life filled with joy and comfort

☐ **EXPERTISE** to attain skills and knowledge in many areas

☐ **FAME** to become prominent, well known, famous

☐ **FAMILY** to belong to and contribute to a close family relationship

☐ **FREEDOM** to possess freedom of thought and action

☐ **FRIENDSHIP** to belong, to be liked, to be accepted and admired by
others as a friend

☐ INFLUENCE to influence people and events through the force of personality and ability

☐ LOVE to give and receive warmth and understanding, to be involved in close, affectionate relationships

☐ RESPONSIBILITY to honor and accomplish certain fundamental responsibilities

☐ SECURITY to obtain a safe, stable and secure place in life

☐ SELF-ACTUALIZATION to strive to and attain the limits of personal and professional development

☐ SERVICE to help others attain their goals, to serve and support a purpose that supersedes personal desires

☐ SPIRITUALITY to feel that what I'm doing is not just of my own making but is part of something that belongs to a larger creation.

Your priorities differ from your values in that they are usually more immediate and temporary. They are priorities for 12 to 18 months, and they set the focus on your behaviors for that time. If you find yourself always "behind the eight ball," putting out fires, or meandering through life, wondering what happened to time, it's likely you haven't documented and focused on your priorities.

How about doing it now? Focus on these priorities by setting a goal for the top three. For example, if one of my priorities is **Friendship** (to belong, to be liked, to be accepted and admired by others as a friend), what goal(s) can I set to be a good friend to someone?

- Make sure I stay in touch regularly?
- Plan a movie night together?

- Invite them to my home for lunch?
- Ask them to join my book club?
- Offer to babysit so they can have a much-needed break?

Knowing Your Own Truths
What Are They?

List three things your teachers told you that you believe that may not necessarily be true.

1. _____

2. _____

3. _____

List three things your parents told you that you believe that may not necessarily be true.

1. _____

2. _____

3. _____

List three things society tells you that you believe that may not necessarily be true.

1. _____

2. _____

3. _____

Write down three of your own beliefs that you have developed that may not be true.

1. _____

2. _____

3. _____

Are these beliefs

- Out of date?
- Invasive?
- Relevant to you today?

I remember when I joined the big corporate world, after running my own "shop" for years, how hard it was for me to get beyond the "shoulds." I really expected everyone to work at my pace, my speed, and with my type of energy. I alienated a lot of people by making them feel "less than" (which, of course, wasn't what I intended), but because I didn't know myself and my beliefs, my behavior was automatic and naturally "always right." Oh, how wrong is that!

Find out what fishbowl you and your upbringing have put you in, so that you can choose to get out of it and be more relaxed and open with yourself today. Let go of the snapshot of "shoulds" and replace it with a wide screen movie of "possibles" and "coulds." You will be much kinder to yourself and those around you … and also more fun!

You did what you knew how to do, and when you knew better, you did better.

— MAYA ANGELOU

How Did You Get Between The Dog And The Fire Hydrant?

Let's spend some time talking about the results of your priorities and values charts. How much of you do you own? How much do you blame others or karma for what goes wrong in your life today?

Anytime we blame, we are giving away our power.

— JULIA B. COLWELL

C'mon now, 'fess up. When you look at your relationships that aren't perfect—relationships with your boss, your siblings, your lover(s), husband/wife, friends—where are you in all this? I know, I know… The boss is a pain. Your mother/father is difficult. Your siblings have lives of their own and don't care about you. Your friends let you down. Generally speaking, people walk all over you, or take advantage of your kindness or generosity of spirit. You're the one always organizing family gatherings, parent/teacher fundraisers, employee get-togethers, buying the holiday gifts. And you resent it. There's a slow burn in your gut, and a feeling of not being appreciated.

Who do you blame for this situation? There's always someone or something. Rarely do we own our own "stuff."

The first question for you is: Who made you general manager of the world? Who said you *had* to do these things, be there, carry the load?

It's time to own it. To own you. Ready?

Action Chart

For each category of your life, list the top four or five actions that you think you need to take to improve your relationship with yourself.

	Personal	Family	Career	Spiritual
1.				
2.				
3.				
4.				
5.				

You And Yourself

Late Fragment

*And did you get what
you wanted from this life, even so?
I did.
And what did you want?
To call myself beloved, to feel myself
beloved on the earth.*

— RAYMOND CARVER

To truly know yourself, you have to know where you are in all aspects of your life because in reality we take ourselves everywhere we go! Many people change countries, careers, husbands/wives because they're not happy or are discontented with their lot, only to find that the same feeling pervades their new job, partnership, or country. When I first came to Canada from England, there were many immigrants who returned "home" to their old country after discovering the new place didn't meet their expectations. Then, six months later, they came back to Canada; it was called the $2,000 cure. We take ourselves everywhere we go—the good and not so good.

That's why it's important to find out, before you venture into relationship land, who you really are, and how you are.

For example, see where you stand on the following Wheel of Life.

Wheel Of Life Balance

How satisfied are you in each area of your life? See the center of the wheel as 0 and the outer edge as 10 (with 0 being the lowest score and 10 the highest) and draw a straight or curved line to create a new outer edge.

Write the number you assign to each section, i.e., Health & Fitness may rank 7 out of 10. Career may be 3 out of 10. Where you draw your lines is the new perimeter of your Wheel of Life Balance as you see it today.

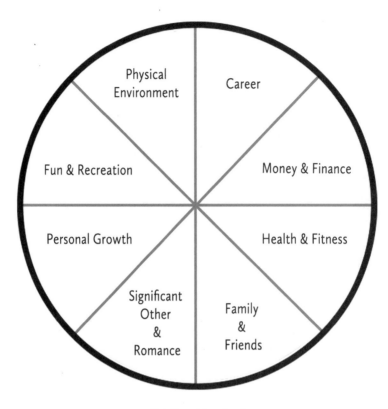

Relationship wheel

Look to see where the scores are low. Check them against the other information you've received from the previous Priorities and Values charts and see what aha's you get! So, for example, if you gave Personal Growth a score of 3, yet listed Self-Actualization (to strive and attain the limits of personal and professional development) as one of your priorities and being a good person as one of your values, then you haven't thought it through and you need to re-evaluate what you mean by "being a good person."

Aha! 1. _____

Aha! 2. _____

Aha! 3. _____

Now you're getting closer to having a relationship with yourself and understanding your true self.

Vision And Goal Clarification Protocol

What do you really, *really* want in your life right now? Here's a way to find out when you're not sure.

1. Get clear on the situation at hand

You need context before you can decide what you want. (One thing at a time, please.)

- Is this about work?
- A relationship?
- Self-actualization?

2. Imagine fantastic, outrageous success

Go on, amp it up. See it clearly, brighten the picture, hear the applause you get from achieving your goal, feel how it feels to be successful … and double that feeling.

What would total and fabulous success look like? Don't get caught up in the "How would I get there?" dilemma. Just focus on what outrageous success looks like—for you.

This process helps you reach for the stars.

3. Clarify your minimum level of success

This allows you realistic stations along the way toward your ultimate goal. This is the bottom line, the "if nothing else, then at least this." Make sure the bottom line really is just that. This is the very least that is acceptable to you.

4. Close your eyes and go inside your imaginative space

Find the sweet spot of what you want, what feels good between those two end points. Sit with it for just a moment, and imagine as clearly as possible what it is you want, what it looks like, feels like, sounds like. Then in your mind and body, double the feeling or visual.

5. Lock it in—in any way that works for you

It may be a single word like "OK" or a signal like "thumbs up."

Now that you've found out more about yourself than you could ever imagine, take a moment and stretch your arms above your head with palms facing each other. That's right, stre-e-e-etch. Now clap your hands together up there. Give yourself a round of applause! You deserve it! You've done more work on self-exploration than most people do in a lifetime! Celebrate!

You can now choose your next steps. Do you need help in some areas of your life? Find that help, whether it's a coach, counselor, hypnotist, regression therapist, psychologist—whatever works for you.

Make it happen. If being a good person is your goal, how do you go about being a better person? Make a list.

- Volunteer at a local hospital.
- Become a dog walker at the Humane Society.
- Take the neighborhood kids to the zoo.
- Raise funds for a good cause.
- Visit your grandmother more often.

It's your life. You're the author of the book of this life, so start manifesting the best you!

> *One ... remember to look up at the stars and not down at your feet. Two ... never give up work. Work gives you meaning and purpose and life is empty without it. Three ... if you are lucky enough to find love, remember it is there and don't throw it away.*
>
> — PROFESSOR STEPHEN HAWKING

Set goals for change. Notice your behaviors in all relationships, starting with the cashier at the supermarket, your boss, your parents, friends, and lovers. And notice what you bring to these relationships now that you understand who you are. And celebrate. Yes, again. And again! And always.

Remember to frequently ask yourself the following questions:

- What are my concerns today about this relationship?
- Is there something I need to do right away to correct it?
- If not right away, when?
- What do I really want from this relationship?
- How do I keep this relationship healthy?
- What did I do today that seemed to improve the relationship?
- Did my actions enhance and enrich the relationship in the long term?

Key Learnings

- It's *your* view of *your* world – it's not *the* world.
- You get to choose who and how you are.
- Everyone is everything. Smart, stupid, kind, unkind, open minded, closed minded, and so on. It's the pieces you choose to use of yourself each day that make you the person you are and the life you live.

Worksheets For This Chapter

✔ Life Values
✔ Priorities
✔ Knowing Your Truths
✔ Action Table
✔ Wheel of Life
✔ Vision and Goal Clarification Protocol

SECTION ONE

—

Family

CHAPTER 3

You and Your Siblings

Siblings are the people we practice on, the people who teach us about fairness and cooperation and kindness and caring, quite often the hard way.

— PAMELA DUGDALE

From the time we are born, our brothers and sisters are our collaborators, co-conspirators, and our role models. They can be our protectors, our tormentors, our playmates, our sources of envy or pride. Along with good guidance from parents, they can help us learn how to resolve conflicts or not. Whatever your circumstance, it's worth considering harmony, no matter whether you reside somewhere on the spectrum of unconditional love or can't stand being around them! They are, like it or not, your soul mate(s) and are here to teach you, or allow you to learn one of the lessons you came into this life to accomplish: forgiveness, compassion, patience, understanding, responsibility, unconditional love, and so on.

When you think about your brother(s) and/or sister(s), what's the image you have of them? What do you see in your mind's eye, what words do you hear or feel in your body when their name comes up, or when you know you're going to be seeing them? Bossy? Distant? Caring? Nosy? Drama Queen (or King)? Complainer/victim? Aggressive? Loving? Combative?

Our siblings push buttons that cast us in roles we felt sure we had let go of long ago—the baby, the peacekeeper, the caretaker, the avoider.... It doesn't seem to matter how much time has elapsed or how far we've traveled.

— JANE MERSKY LEDER

Let me ask you some questions about these feelings, and you might want to make notes of your answers. It will help with the changes you want to make.

- How much is this feeling left over from your relationship growing up with them?
- Where are you in the birth order?
- Did you ever feel that one sibling was more favored than the other? Was it you?
- Were you closer to your mom or your dad?
- Are your parents still together? If not, how old were you when they separated?
- How did you find out about the separation?
- Did you or one of your siblings take over the role of missing parent when that happened?
- How have your relationships changed—if at all—since then?

The reason for these questions is that we are inclined to take mental snapshots of people we've known for a long time, and never more so than when we are young. The older brother is expected to "take charge" and be the success beacon in the family, and, if he doesn't, the family feels let down. The youngest is used to being the baby, to being taken care of and rescued when they get into mischief. Often they are the charmers or entertainers in the family—the funny one, the adult relative the kids love to be around.

For more information on this aspect of family dynamics as it relates to birth order, check out *The New Birth Order* by Kevin Leman; you'll be surprised by how "right on" it is. Of course, there are always exceptions to the rule, and you may be one of those exceptions. But bottom line, it should help you see how your relationship with your siblings is working, and if it's stuck, where is it stuck?

How parents interact with each child as he or she enters the
family circle determines in great part that child's final destiny.

— KEVIN LEMAN, *THE BIRTH ORDER BOOK*

How much of that feeling is left over from sharing your childhood with your sibling? Are you seeing them as the person they are today? Are you "feeling" how they made you feel when you were a kid? Automatic family responses are part of our life more than we realize.

Who hasn't experienced the dread of family gatherings, knowing how each person will behave? Dad will belittle number one son; Sis will be giggly and flirtatious, not taking anything seriously; and Mom will be the victim/martyr, eating after everyone else has been served, saying how the food wasn't cooked enough or too much.

Old jokes. Old stories. Old reactions. Old rivalries. And as the parents take on their role with the snapshot of "the kids" being children, so you and your siblings bicker and tease and go right back to being eight or 10 years old again. It happens all the time. Sometimes more covertly than others, but we fall back into patterns of childhood when we are with multi generations of family—or even just two generations.

To the outside world, we all grow old. But not to brothers and
sisters. We know each other as we always were. We know each
other's hearts. We share private family jokes. We remember
family feuds and secrets, family griefs and joys. We live outside
the touch of time.

— CLARA ORTEGA

If you've been raised in a home where everyone yells, where there's constant criticism, your subconscious mind will accept that as appropriate and "normal." And it will become your default approach to all relationships: challenging, confrontational, and maybe negative. You won't even realize you're doing it! But you don't have to be locked in. The good news is, if you recognize that your imprinting as a child needn't shape the adult you are today, you're 80 percent home. The bad news? The other 20 percent takes more work!!

> *You can't change what you don't acknowledge.*
>
> — PHILLIP C. MCGRAW (DR. PHIL)

Because of the value a healthy relationship with a sibling can bring to your life, the lives of your children, and the family in general, it's worth working on it to bring your perception and experience of the relationship up to date and keep it healthy.

So, how do we bring our snapshots up to date, so that we are comfortable as adults with our siblings? As with all relationships, we need to look at the expectations we have of our siblings and the relationships with them; we also need to move beyond the "I wish" to "It just is."

We expect them to take us the way we are, so let's find a way to take them the way they are.

> *No one has the power to make me suffer but me. It is my opinion about whatever the situation is, or what it is the other person is doing, or not doing, that is the source of my suffering. It is not what they do, or not do; it is what I think about it.*
>
> — BYRON KATIE

Ready to do some work?

Siblings Dynamic

(Explain in detail under each heading: Physical, Emotional, and Intellectual)

When I was...	My relationship with my brother/sister was...		
	Physical	Emotional	Intellectual
Under 10.			
A teenager			
In my 20s			
And now			
I recognize these old patterns and want to change to this . . .			
In the future			
So that my relationship with my sibling(s) looks and feels like this . . .			
From now on			

Now, let's take a closer look at what angers, disappoints, or confuses you.

- What is it about them you don't like?
- How do you want them to change?
- What do you need from them in order to feel more comfortable in the relationship?
- What is it you don't want to experience in your relationship with them?

To get there, we need to go back to basics. Let's look at what is really important to you and your relationships. What are your values?

Relationship with Your Siblings – Your Values

List your key six or eight Life Values. Be honest; no point in pretending here. Maybe you have only four or six key values. List them in any order.

1. _____

2. _____

3. _____

4. _____

5. _____

6. _____

7. _____

8. _____

How can you use these values to get to where you want to be? For instance, if Kindness or Caring is one of your values, how can you manifest it in a way that will work for you in the relationship with your siblings, while also keeping your Self-respect and Boundaries? What will you do to make the changes and plan for positive outcomes?

Consider treating your siblings as you do your friends—always assuming, of course, that you treat your friends well!!

Well done is better than well said.

— BENJAMIN FRANKLIN

Allow them to be who and how they are, and love and respect them anyway. How they behave in their own life really has nothing to do with you, unless of course it damages your life in some way. (Think about that for a moment; it could bring a huge aha!)

How are you going to bring your values into the relationships you have with your sibs?

Look over your values, and make a plan—a map—of the new territory. Think about and plan around the hills and valleys of your relationships. Where you are both in sunlight, and where you are in the shade. Where you want to put in some more light, and where you need more space. The key to success in this protocol is to understand that you are the one making the change. And you're making it for yourself, not the other person. You're making the change so that you can have family in your life, and family is frequently messy. It's *never* tidy, and it's never exactly the way we want it to be!

> *Sibling relationships—and 80 percent of Americans have at least one—outlast marriages, survive the death of parents, resurface after quarrels that would sink any friendship. They flourish in a thousand incarnations of closeness and distance, warmth, loyalty, and distrust.*
>
> — ERICA E. GOODE

Also, all changes have a trajectory, whether they are about diet, learning a new language, or a new behavior. Ask any sports coach and they will tell you, there's always a blip. And it looks something like this:

As you can see, downward blips happen—always. But it's worth remembering that if you regard it just as a blip, and not the end of the process (*it's just not working*) and keep at it, you'll start again, after the blip, from a higher level than before.

Also, when changing the interaction between two people, and understanding that it's only you that can do the actual changing (because you want to), the pattern usually looks like this:

My action	Timing	Result
I initiate the change	1 month	none
Maintain	1–3 months	awareness/resistance
Fall back , tired of trying	4–5 months	awareness/resistance
Renew efforts	5–8 months	awareness/sporadic
Fall back, habit	8–9 months	reach out/sporadic

This is just a general idea, but what happens when we make a change is that it takes a while for the other person to notice. Then they have to decide if and how to react to what they are noticing. They will wait to see if they can trust the change. Then they make the overtures to change from their point of view—*as much as they are able*—and if they want the relationship.

Priorities With My Sibling Relationship
(Rank in order of importance to you)

☐ ACHIEVEMENT

☐ AUTHORITY

☐ ENJOYMENT – FUN

☐ FAMILY

☐ FREEDOM

☐ FRIENDSHIP

☐ LOVE

☐ RESPONSIBILITY

☐ SELF-ACTUALIZATION

These priorities relate directly to building and managing the relationship you've inherited, and to being able to maintain your integrity and boundaries but also open to new ways of looking at and behaving toward your siblings. You want family.

How about doing it now? Focus on these priorities by setting a goal for the top three. My top three priorities are:

1. _____

2. _____

3. _____

And this is the process and timing for each one (*What I will do by when?*):

1. _____

2. _____

3. _____

Now you're on your way to having a manageable relationship with your siblings. It may not be the stuff that television families are made of, but it's real, and you can live with it … and maybe even enjoy it! Adding in the giggle factor, if you can, as a bonus gold star.

And on the way, don't forget to ask yourself the following questions:

- How do I keep this relationship healthy?
- What did I do today that seemed to improve the relationship?
- Did my actions enhance and enrich the relationship in the long term?
- What are my concerns about this relationship?
- What do I really want from this relationship?

Key Learnings

- Who we were isn't who we are.
- People change (they're not still crawling on the ground or wearing diapers).
- Unconditional love is just that—no conditions on acceptance. We just are, and they just are.
- The sibling relationship needs constant monitoring to keep the relationship circle current and up to date.
- Our siblings are our partners in living, from birth onward. We can enjoy and use that comfort of the familiar, or abuse and ignore it, knowing that the latter encourages a deep-felt loneliness

Worksheets for this chapter

✔ Sibling Questionnaire
✔ Siblings Dynamic
✔ Life Values
✔ Priorities

CHAPTER 4

You and Your Spouse for Life

Lovers are such strange people,
they are not like everybody else.
They don't carry their souls in their bodies,
Instead, their souls carry them.

— RUMI

(Caveat – All client names have been changed
for this book unless otherwise stated).

"I knew, the moment I saw him, we were connected."

"I walked into the business meeting, and there he was, sitting behind the desk, and I felt a deep sense of recognition."

"I met her at a friend's dinner party, and we started talking and have never stopped. I never dreamed I could be in love with a woman."

"I'm 75 years old. Who knew this could happen to me at this age. I feel 16 all over again!"

"I met him on J Date, and from the moment we spoke on the phone, we knew there was something there!"

"I love him and he loves me, but we're in different cities, and we're starting to drift apart."

"I can't live with her, and I can't live without her. What's going on here?"

All true, all examples from my clients. Some lasted a few weeks, some have lasted a few years, and others are ongoing. There are two commonalities among all these: one is that sense of "belonging" or destiny, and the other is a non-ownership of the relationship. It just happens.

> *Love is an emotion that keeps you coming home to the same*
> *person every night for years.*
>
> — IRA HYMAN, *THE INFATUATION TRAP*

The trouble with "it just happens," however, is that there is no one at the wheel of the love boat. The relationship just evolves without any thought or consideration of what's next. Sometimes the inevitability of the relationship and its downfall seem to have come from learned behavior. I'm not kidding!

> *Forever is composed of nows.*
>
> — EMILY DICKINSON

Margrit came into the clinic to see if she could find out why she always "found losers." She had been married three times and couldn't understand what she wasn't seeing or doing right. She was dating a man who wanted to marry her, and she wanted to be sure she wasn't making the same mistake again.

I had some investigative discussions with her about her expectations around marriage and relationships, and both she and I discovered, to her surprise, that she hadn't really thought about it; she just knew she was attracted to this type of man and wanted to be with them all the time. In her words, she felt the deep instant connection, both intellectually and sexually. "It's strange to say it, but we are instantly familiar with each other's minds and our bodies." On further investigation, she explained her family structure growing up.

"Dad wasn't around much, and I missed him a lot because we were really connected. I didn't feel that way with my mom. In fact, I spent all my days, from as far back as I can remember, waiting for my dad to come home." She started to cry. "I'm realizing now, I only felt I existed when he was home.

He loved me more than my brother and sister. When he was home, we did everything together."

"How often was he home?" I asked.

"He worked as a consultant for an engineering company, so traveled quite a bit, sometimes for a month at a time. I would pile up things to show him, like my artwork from school or report cards. I literally put my life on hold for him," she said, startled at her realization. "I realize now I barely breathed or lived when he wasn't there."

When I asked about her mother, she said, "My mother just accepted it, like she accepted my father's absence. She focused more on my younger brother and sister and is still closer to them."

She went on to explain that the atmosphere in the house was "efficient." The kids were well taken care of. "We didn't need for anything. Music, sports, gymnastics—whatever we wanted to do, we did."

When I pressed her for the emotional atmosphere in the home, she couldn't recall anything other than "It was efficient. We were taken care of and well fed."

I gave her some homework—the same as I've given you: Values and Priorities—and booked her for a follow-up session the following week.

For her second session, Margrit was eager to tell me about the abandonment dreams she'd had in the week since our session. I explained that it's not unusual to connect more through dreams once you start working with the subconscious mind. And working through her values and priorities, and how she was currently in harmony with them (or not), would give us some clues as to whether she was abandoning herself or always getting ready to emotionally abandon another person—always one foot out the door, knowingly or unknowingly. This subconscious message could be the key to her relationship issues.

A 2011 study published in the Journal of Applied Social Psychology *showed that the more one's self-worth depends on a relationship, the more suffering one is likely to feel when it's over.*

— LISA A. PHILIPS

The Third Circle Loving Partner Protocol

After completing the Priorities and Values assignment, Margrit understood more about herself. I explained to her that by using the Values worksheet and understanding the bedrock on which she stands, she also set her boundaries. Lovers can't know your boundaries unless you know them yourself! Values, by and large, stay with us for most of our life.

Margrit's Life Values

Without a strong relationship and understanding of self, it's virtually impossible to have a strong and deep lasting relationship with others – any sort of relationship. We have to know who we are before we know what we want/need/can offer in a relationship with another person. Here are Margrit's Life Values, as written on her worksheet.

List your key six or eight Life Values (be honest; no point in pretending here). These are the bedrock of where you stand in life—what is truly important to you. Maybe you have only four or six key values, but list them in any order.

1. Fun
2. Freedom
3. Trust
4. Honesty
5. Respect
6. Commitment
7. Security
8. Safety

Margrit then committed to giving the Values worksheet to Tony, so they could start the dialogue of looking forward to a shared life with the same, similar, or dissimilar values. The key here is to know whether you are alike in this foundation, or different, and to understand that if your values are very different, then it's unlikely a relationship will flourish.

At this point, Margrit reassessed her priorities, with the idea of working toward becoming an active partner in the relationship with Tony, without compromising her sense of self. This thoughtful process was an anomaly for her (*"I'm not used to thinking this much about myself and what I want"*), and it allowed her to discover the potential for her own space, place, and responsibility in a relationship.

Margrit's Priorities

The Priorities worksheet represents where you will choose to spend your time and focus over the next 6–12 months. It enables you to clarify the short-term version of the changes you want to make or the goals you want to achieve. Margrit also agreed to give this sheet to Tony for his list of priorities.

Achievement	
Affluence	
Authority	
Enjoyment	5
Expertise	
Fame	
Family	6
Freedom	2
Friendship	3
Influence	
Love	4
Responsibility	
Security	
Self-actualization	1
Service / Spirituality	

Needs – Wants – Gives

We [he and wife Jools] love each other to bits, but I don't think marriage is easy.

— JAMIE OLIVER, *CELEBRITY CHEF*

The next step toward consciously shaping their relationship is for both parties to answer the following questions:

- What do I *need* from my relationship?
- What do I *want* from my relationship?
- What am I prepared to *give* to the relationship?

I always suggest that these be worked on separately and then sent or brought to me so that we can work together on the blueprint or "contract" for the relationship: the Third Circle. This allows the rush of love to exist and flourish while remembering to honor each person's own authenticity. Then, together, they can focus on keeping that Third Circle—the Relationship Circle— healthy, vibrant, and strong, whatever else is going on in their separate worlds. Work or family tension becomes easier to handle without impacting the Relationship Circle. Again, this shows areas where they are together on their vision of moving forward, and where there may be differences.

As Margrit and Tony worked on these important questions, they realized that they were coming from totally different points of view of what an ongoing relationship could or would be. They decided to part, the best of friends but not lovers or partners. And Margrit, for the first time in her life, began to understand who she really is, and what she wanted and would look for in future loving relationships.

Many people don't feel like working on their relationship. You might think it all seems too hard or it's pointless, or you shouldn't have to, or the fault is all with your partner. The problem is, if you're not willing to work on your relationship,

then you're effectively choosing to prolong your difficulties or
make them even worse. So if this is where you are at right now,
then take [the time] to notice what this attitude is costing you.

— RUSS HARRIS, *ACT WITH LOVE*

To "own" your part in any relationship, you have to know, in your mind, what that relationship should be, feel, and behave like for you. What is your view of the world of your ideal relationship? And by the way, this applies to all relationships: with your family, your job, your friends, and your lovers.

What is in the contract of your ideal relationship—usually unrecognized until it's too late? What do you **need** (non-negotiable), what do you **want** (preferable), and what are you prepared to **give** to your relationships?

These three words (need, want, give), operating within the environment of Values and Priorities, are the architectural drawing of your relationships. This format becomes your blueprint for all interactions beyond that of cashier at the checkout counter. And even then…

Once you have worked this through, you will choose more wisely and behave differently, knowing that you have set your standards for thriving relationships. So why would you let yourself down?

The best relationship is one in which partners not only actively
repair regrettable incidents—but do so quickly

— JOHN GOTTMAN

Wherever You Go, There You Are!

Lesley and Jay met online and there was an instant connection. Within six weeks, Jay had to move to another city for business, but they were committed to keeping the relationship alive and thriving.

I explained to them that we needed to look at their relationship as a separate entity from the two of them, and that it needed to be fed and nurtured to stay vibrant and healthy. I showed them what that would look like for each of them. I also gave them an example from another couple—who happened to be gay and older—to show what the outcome could look like:

Relationship Contract

The loving partner relationship I choose to live and grow with contains:

- Acknowledgment and focus that our relationship comes first before individual wants or old habits
- Time and space for physical health and exercise
- Time for culture – music and the arts
- Time for friends – mostly together but sometimes separately
- Honesty and fidelity at all times
- Kindness and respect at all times
- Emotional intimacy and trust
- Financial responsibility and accountability
- Responsibility and accountability for where and how we live
- Love and responsibility for our animals
- A clean and tidy home

Lesley and Jay did their homework and their charts looked like this:

Lesley's Life Values	Jay's Life Values
Loyalty	Happiness
Love	Family
Compassion	Acceptance
Wisdom	Love
Dependability	Entertainment
Kindness	Making people happy
Honesty	
Empathy	

Priorities

Lesley's Top 5 Priorities	Jay's Top 5 Priorities
Enjoyment	Happiness
Freedom	Security
Security	Responsibility
Responsibility	Self-actualization
Influence	Service

Lesley and Jay then worked on their Needs, Wants, and Give worksheets to develop the Relationship Circle.

Needs & Wants

Lesley's Needs	Jay's Needs	Lesley's Wants	Jay's Wants
Trust	Love	Excitement	A friend 24×7
Loyalty	Respect	Commitment	
Dependability	Same goals	Honesty	
Companionship	Empathy	Tolerance	
Understanding		Openness	
Patience			
Order			
Love			

Gives

Lesley's Gives	Jay's Gives
Commitment	Myself, completely
Trust	To be there 24×7 for the relationship
Loyalty	
Stability	
Love	
Companionship	

As you can see, although the answers were different in some places, the core values were the same. So together we built their Relationship Blueprint—the Third Circle—which looked like this:

- *We* come first
- Joy
- Love
- Trust
- Respect
- Honesty
- Loyalty
- Listening
- Laughter
- Nurturing
- Acceptance
- Total support
- Dependability
- Romantic time
- Financial security
- Physical intimacy
- Friends time

They took this away with them and worked out the details that they could both commit to, i.e., how much time alone with friends; what exactly "financial security" looked like to both of them; and another level they had developed: their own personal goal sheets to keep the Third Circle vibrant and healthy.

Forgiveness And Creating
A Forgiveness Ritual

The most important thing in communication is to hear what isn't being said.

— PETER DRUCKER

In every relationship, and I mean *every* relationship, something always goes wrong. One person makes a mistake—or ignores feelings or unspoken agreements. If ignored, this incident can cause resentment and an eventual crack in the circle, even possibly a total break.

One way of circumventing this breakdown of the Relationship Circle is through agreement, ritual, and understanding, and a total buy-in from both parties without game playing or sulks. Yes, unfortunately adults do sulk!

Do the work separately, but come together to complete the ritual.

STEP 1: Complete these three sentences

The thoughts, feelings, and memories I've been holding onto are

_____

Holding onto all this has hurt our relationship in the following ways

_____

I want to build a better relationship, based on the following values

_____

Use the Values worksheet and Priorities worksheet at the end of this book (see Addenda on page 162) to set your blueprint for moving forward.

STEP 2: Write your own "letting go" commitment.

My commitment is to

_____

STEP 3: Choose a special place to read your answers to each other.

As the person reads their commitment, it is received in silence and with loving, full attention. This is no time for "yes buts" or "I already do that" comments. This is truly listening—heart and soul listening.

STEP 4: Celebrate starting over.

Do something, right away, not next week, or when we have time. Do it NOW! Hug. Burn the letters. Go for a walk. Watch a funny movie. Go for a special dinner.

What About That "Instant Connection" Bit?

Never make someone a priority when all you are to them is an option.

— MAYA ANGELOU

My belief is that when a baby is born, it is a new, fresh soul coming into this world, expecting to be loved unconditionally and nurtured as the wonderful God-given being that it is. However, if the child is born into a family that is emotionally distant—or discordant; abusive physically, emotionally, or sexually; addictive in some way; or living in drama—then that gets stamped into the subconscious mind as love. It becomes what the child expects. So throughout life, we are inclined to choose friends, lovers, and partners who somehow reflect what we received emotionally at birth, which is why many people go from abusive relationship to abusive relationship, one after the other, without knowing why.

> Why do we take part in others' dramas, even when we recognize
> that we are acting in a script that does not suit us? We do so
> because of the deep, unconscious, and terribly painful fear that
> if we are not enacting what others need, we will cease to exist for
> them at all… For the person in an abusive relationship, it is better
> to endure abuse than not to exist at all.
>
> — RUTHELLEN JOSSELSON, JASON ARONSON

Somewhere, deep in the subconscious mind, we feel "comfortable" with the energy being given off. Even if it's well hidden, it still seems familiar. We believe we are meeting someone who is like us, someone who will understand us, someone we can love.

This is the perfect time and place to use the Third Circle Protocol, because it brings considered thought into play, releasing old relationship patterns and habits, and allowing movement forward into healthy, supportive, respectful, and loving relationships.

Appreciating Your Partner

Fill in this form each day. Notice (at least) three things you appreciate about your partner. They don't have to be big things—they might be the way he smiles or the sound of her laughter.

3 Things I noticed today that I appreciate about my partner	3 Ways my partner contributed to my life today	3 Things my partner said or did today that represent their best strengths and qualities
1.	1.	1.
2.	2.	2.
3.	3.	3.

And remember to ask yourself the following questions:

- How do I keep this relationship healthy?
- What did I do today that seemed to improve the relationship?
- Did my actions enhance and enrich the relationship in the long term?
- What are my concerns about this relationship?
- What do I really want from this relationship?
- Is there something I need to do right away to correct it?
- If not right away, when?

Key Learnings

- Shared values are important for any long-term relationship.
- It's not about you versus me; it's about the relationship.
- Focus on keeping the Relationship Contract vibrant and healthy.
- You're both on the same side!

Worksheets For This Chapter

✔ Life Values
✔ Priorities
✔ Needs – Wants – Gives
✔ Forgiveness Ritual
✔ Appreciating Your Partner

CHAPTER 5

You and Your Kids

*You can clutch the past so tightly to your chest that it leaves
your arms too full to embrace the present.*

— JAN GLIDEWELL

■ **"What the heck just happened here?"**

I wonder how many parents have said that about their kids when overnight they a) changed from being sweet, fun, and lighthearted to sullen, withdrawn, noncommunicative, and rude, or b) stay close to the family until they are married, then suddenly disappear—no phone calls, no visits, no popping in for a hug. Yup, things and people change, including our kids. The old unwritten contract—or Third Circle—isn't working anymore. Most often it takes a while to accept that, in fact, things have changed. We think, or hope, it's just an aberration and everything will go back to the way it was before the door slam, or the forgotten birthday.

But it doesn't. And it can get worse. Much worse. And of course, we're living the old contract while they have moved on to the new. It's likely that your old contract included words like obedience, good manners (whatever that means to you), believing everything I say is correct, true, and absolute. (You might not actually *say* that, but that's the expectation of most parents toward their young child.) And the child, of course, has you on a pedestal, believing all that. And then suddenly, they don't!!

*When one door closes another door opens, but we so often look
so long and so regretfully upon the closed door that we do not
see the ones which open for us.*

— ALEXANDER GRAHAM BELL

65

Whatever the age of our child or children, we have to decide if we want to be right, or do we want to be loving and loved. And that ain't easy.

First we need to look at the contracts we have with them—and if we're honest, they're full of "shoulds." Everything from homework to picking up after themselves to phoning every day to see how you are, or bringing the grandchildren over to see you every week, at least once. All of this, of course, engenders negative self-talk. There may even be some self-destructive self-talk (*Where did I go wrong as a parent that this is happening?* or *I'm a failure as a parent. I should be able to connect with them better. I should probably never have had kids*).

As these situations are inclined to go on for years, if not caught and changed, the negative self-talk can continue (*It's never going to get better. I'm obviously not equipped to handle this. They're moving away from me. They don't need/want me anymore*). Or with teenagers who have suddenly become rude and disrespectful, the self-talk might sound like: *She/he's going through a phase; maybe if I ignore it, it will stop.*

> *If you quickly make yourself overly upset about these things by awfulizing and shoulding, you will soon be part of the problem. Again, your appropriate alternative is not to roll over and say, "So what? Who cares?" but to think in terms of preferences: "I'd like to figure these directions out quickly, but it may take some time."*
>
> — ALBERT ELLIS, PH.D. & ARTHUR LANGE, ED.D.

Among the many emotions we feel about this, the overriding emotion is one of loss of connection. The heart connection is somehow disconnected, and the more we make them "wrong," the more disconnected we become. So-o-o-o...

Back to the list of Needs, Wants, and Gives. In the light of the new circumstances in which you find yourself, maybe it's time to revisit and rewrite these. I strongly suggest that any wording that even vaguely suggests "obey" be discarded.

Why is it that I can hear you saying right about now, "But this isn't real life. It's not that easy." You're right. It's not easy. But it does work—unless, of course, you talk yourself out of it. I have had countless successes with this in the clinic with families facing these issues. The key here is to know it's solvable, and to continue being loved instead of being right.

So let's look to see what your new contract might look like.

Your Needs, Wants, And Gives

Because we're looking at change and managing that change, we need to know where we are now and where we want to go. Take a sheet of paper and write down the answers to both sets of questions. Now and for the future. Take your time; your family's emotional future depends on your considered thought, right now!

First, think about your current contract—the one you formulated a while ago, the one that's not working now.

- What did you *need* in the beginning—the words and feelings you felt that were non-negotiable at that time?
- What did you *want*—in the way of performance, interaction, and responsibility?
- What were you prepared to *give* to your child, including, I hope, unconditional love?

Once you've done that, start thinking about how things need to change as your child matures and pulls away from parental control.

To predetermine success, you might also want to discuss this whole process with your child. Tell them you realize that circumstances have changed and that you're looking at your expectations of them and their behavior and bringing them more in line with the current situation. And then, when you've done that, let them know you'd like to talk to them about your new expectations, and would like them to do the same process so that you're both on the same page. Guess what? About 99 percent of the time you'll get a positive response, once they know that you're changing first, and you're going to run these suggested changes past them for their buy-in. Then they'll feel more confident in doing theirs for you.

Your New Contract

What are your needs, must haves?

_____

_____

(Respectful language and interaction? Honesty? Calm discussion? Respect as a person? To be heard? Kindness?)

What are your wants? Preferences? Nice to haves?

_____

_____

(Some fun alone time with them, shopping, a movie, and so on? Phone or Skype calls regularly?) Whatever works for you is a "nice to have."

What will you give to the relationship?

_____

_____

(Unconditional love: what does that mean to you and how does it look or manifest itself? Nonjudgmental listening. More space to make their own decisions: for younger kids, as long as you know what they are. Later bedtimes or curfews on weekends—or whatever you know they want and you can happily live with.)

Then list your Values and Priorities (see Appendix for sheets).

Tina and her mother Laurel came to see me because they were at an impasse about 17-year-old Tina taking a year off after high school before going on to college or university. Tina had heard me talk about the Third Circle Protocol on the radio and felt it would help move things forward for her and her mother.

I could see that Laurel was very uncomfortable about the whole situation and, when I asked her why, she replied that she didn't really appreciate her daughter dragging their personal discussions out in public. "It's family business, and I don't know why she won't listen to me about this. I'm not an old dodo. I know what's going on in the world. University is important, and jobs aren't easy to find."

She crossed her arms and sat, waiting for me to disagree. I could see and feel that she was angry and felt disrespected by her daughter and possibly me.

My first step was to agree with her. "You are absolutely correct. Education is important. And jobs are not easy to find. I can totally understand where you're coming from."

I then told them both that I had a daughter who at one time wanted to leave school, which she did, but eventually went back—her own decision—and got her PhD.

"Yes, it was troubling at the time," I confirmed, "but we realized that if we forced her to stay in school, she could be there in body but not in spirit or focus. And there are millions of ways to goof off at university, if the person doesn't want to study," I added.

They both agreed—Tina with a grin and Laurel not so much!

After suggesting an exercise to see if they could come to mutual ground, I asked them to work with me on their list of relationship Values and Priorities (see Appendix). Laurel initially wanted to know what that had to do with her daughter's going to university. I had to be careful with this one. If Tina hadn't been there, I would have asked her if she would prefer to be right or to be loved, but I didn't want to put Laurel on the spot in front of her daughter. Using the Values and Priorities system allowed them both to save face.

Let's talk about saving face for a moment. Saving face for both parties is critical when working with two opposing factions, even more so with parents and children because, at some point during their relationship, from about seven years of age onwards, the relationship often changes, as they move from admiration/caring to adversarial/commanding. My goal and role with the Third Circle protocol is to shift that, to move it to a mutual contract that both parties can live with for at least the next six months; six months is a long time for a kid!

> *People in relationships must be able to influence each other.*
> *There is a big difference between influence (which happens*
> *when we speak from our emotional being) and control (when*
> *we get parental).*
>
> — JULIA B. COWELL

I explained to them both that, beyond everything else, their relationship as mother and daughter was precious, and we wanted to be sure it stayed that way. Relationships change over time—they all do—but we want to be sure that the core of love and respect stays consistent throughout time. They were both surprised that they hadn't thought of themselves that way.

Laura commented that "this could probably help with the other kids, too." I explained further that all relationships are an unwritten contract, and sometimes one person changes that contract and throws out the expected pattern of behavior without warning, which makes everyone at best uncomfortable, and at worst feeling confused and angry.

Both Laurel and Tina took time out and wrote out their eight to 10 Values and list of Priorities over the next six to 12 months. I saw them separately for their next appointment so we could work through their part of the new contract without pretense or worry that the other person might be offended or critical of their choices.

Laurel dropped Tina off at the clinic and said she'd be back in an hour to pick her up. Tina was excited about the appointment, telling me that it was the first real grown-up thing she'd done without her mother looking over her shoulder. She said she found it easy since she knew what she wanted. As we went through the process, some of that confidence and ease faded. Like many kids, she hadn't given the questions much considered thought, and had written the answers out of feelings at that moment. It was understandable, considering her age, but not useful in this context of building a new relationship—with herself and her family.

Tina's Values

Respect, Love, Freedom, Family, Fun, Friendship, Travel, Volunteering.

As we worked together to see if she actually applied these values to herself, she began to see some gaps in her belief system about herself, and it caused her to feel embarrassed and uncomfortable.

- Does she respect herself? *"Yes."*
- Does she love herself? *"Yes, but it sort of sounds weird to love yourself."*
- What does she mean by Freedom? And does she use it for herself? For instance, is she freethinking or restricting herself in some way? *On reflection she realized she was quite closed-minded about herself, seeing herself only in one way.*
- What does she do to nurture her friendships? *Lots. "I'm a giver and the organizer in my group."*
- Does she volunteer? It turns out she doesn't but just likes the idea, so it's not really a strong value! *"I will when I have the time."* (As an aside, she didn't like it when I pointed that out. She liked seeing herself that way.)
- Does she travel? Does she make plans to explore countries to go to? *The answer was no! Another "empty" value. "I don't have the*

money to do it, and anyway, my parents wouldn't let me travel without them."

I had to remember that Tina is a teenager and, like most teenagers, she has dreams about what she would like to be and become. Her view of her world isn't mature; the frontal cortex of her brain hasn't been fully formed yet! So we have to work with what she has that is real for her, and for us, at the time. After some discussion about the life values she could live with now, today, and maybe tomorrow, this is what she came up with:

> *Respect. Family. Friends. Love. Fun.*
> These five Values made sense and connected with her in a way she hadn't thought of before. Once we worked through those, Tina felt better about herself. I explained that over the next four or five years, she might find herself adding others, such as Kindness, Honesty, and Curiosity. But for now, we could work with these.

Tina loved this exercise, once she got over the feeling she had "failed the test." It was the first time she had really thought about herself and how she saw her world. We discussed how this was a fantastic base for her future, as she would always be aware of who she was and what she stood for, and no one could ever take that away from her.

(As an aside, I've found this to be a wonderful tool to use with women who have a habit of choosing abusive partners—the earlier we can get this awareness, the better.)

Then came Tina's next six months' priorities. Her top five:

- Self-Actualization – *"I want to find out who I am before I go to university."*
- Service – *"Maybe the way I do that is by volunteering in different places."*

- Family – *"The most important part of my life. I don't want to lose that."*
- Freedom – *"I want to find out who I am and what I want for my future before I go to university."*
- Friendship – *"Most important after my family."*

The bottom four were not surprising, except for the last one:

- Fame
- Expertise
- Authority
- Responsibility

Laurel came right into the office and sat down expectantly. She was excited with the process, hoping to at last connect and understand her daughter's life process. She had realized in the interim that it wasn't the same as her own, and it couldn't be changed with arguments or bribery. She also realized that this was a major opportunity for her to rethink how she would spend the rest of her life, once her children left the home.

Laurel's Values

Family, Love, Respect, Honesty, Education (ongoing learning), the Arts, Friends, the Outdoors.

Laurel's Top Five Priorities

Family, Love, Responsibility, Enjoyment, Security.

Her Bottom Five

Authority, Affluence, Achievement, Expertise, Self-Actualization.

The next step was to give them both homework in order to work on the next segment of the process, but I suggested they do it separately, at home, so we could work on it together at their next combined meeting with me.

When they came back to their next meeting together in the clinic, they were both wary of what they would discover and conscious of the fact that it could be uncomfortable. They had never kept secrets about their feelings from each other before, so it felt a bit strange and awkward for them. Tina was excited and bubbly about the new possible way of interacting with her mom, but Laurel was more guarded, and understandably so.

I told them I would write on the white board what they had brought with them, and together we would craft a new Third Circle relationship contract that they could both agree to and adhere to. I described the protocol as non-critical and accepting. Whatever each person put down was to be accepted without question or quibble, and possibly adjusted later—but not now.

I asked Tina to go first, as it would give her mom time to absorb and adjust a bit to what was on Tina's list before she contributed hers.

Tina

- **NEED:** Love and caring. To be heard. Freedom. Support.
- **WANT:** Laughter. Friendship. Treated like an adult. Space to make mistakes.
- **GIVE:** Love and caring. Promises kept. Fun.

Laurel

- **NEED:** Love. Respect. To be heard. Kindness.
- **WANT:** Fun. Warmth. Responsibilities met.
- **GIVE:** Unconditional love. Support (financial and emotional). Fun. Listening.

As you can see there is some overlap, which is a good thing, but also quite a distance in other areas. After working it through—and it took a couple of appointments in the clinic, with them doing some homework between—this is what they finally came up with, that they could both live with and be happy about.

Our Mother–Daughter
Relationship Contract

- Love, caring, and kindness above all
- Mutual respect
- Listening
- Agreed-to responsibilities met (to be documented monthly)
- New rules and boundaries around freedom to be reviewed and agreed to every four months.

The key to the success of this new contract was that the rules and boundaries around freedom had to be discussed in detail. Yes to a year off for Tina to "find herself"—with commitments for doing something with that time. Volunteer or other work = contribution to society and family. Not lying around the house all day or on the computer. It has to be a productive year, and that would be reviewed every three months in a formal meeting with parents, both the past and a plan for the future three months. Curfews were also discussed.

We arranged for a follow-up meeting four weeks later to see what progress had been made. The school year was over and the first parent-Tina meeting had taken place to set the first three months. Boundaries and curfews set and agreed to. Tina had found some listening-skills tips online and shared them with her parents, and they were all—so far—staying on track.

We agreed that I would be available for Skype or clinic calls if needed in between each three-month period, from either Tina or her parents. In addition, we would have a meeting at the six-month mark to chart progress and make whatever adjustments were needed for the second half of the program. It turned out that Tina's parents came to my clinic and we connected with Tina through Skype because she was volunteering in Tanzania for the month. At this stage of her growth and change, Tina thought she wanted to go back to school and get her Masters in Social Work and study one or two languages as well.

Her father told me after the call that he was hoping she would go into business as an accountant or lawyer, as she was smart and focused. But he realized that she could also bring these skills to her chosen career path, whatever it would be.

Tina is currently at the University of Toronto School of Social Work, ready to move on to postgraduate studies. Laurel is using the Third Circle protocol with her other kids, and checks in with me from time to time for a slight readjustment around language or contract writing for the different personalities in her family.

> *Reality discipline steers a course between an authoritarian style and a permissive style, giving kids some choices but also holding them accountable.*
>
> — KEVIN LEMAN

So with your kids, always remember to ask yourself the following questions:

- How do I keep this relationship healthy?
- Is there something I need to do right away to correct it?
- If not right away, when?
- What did I do today that seemed to improve the relationship?
- Did my actions enhance and enrich the relationship in the long term?
- What are my concerns about this relationship?
- What do I really want from this relationship?

Key Learnings

- Family relationships are probably the most difficult because of the expected roles we play.
- There is a danger of judgment, bullying ("because this is my house, and I said so") and manipulation from both sides.
- Always return to the contract, remembering the goal, short and long term.

Worksheets For This Chapter

✔ Needs – Wants – Gives
✔ Life Values
✔ Priorities

CHAPTER 6

You and Your Aging Parents

When one viewpoint fails to solve a problem, we can adopt other perspectives.

— MARVIN MINSKY, *THE SOCIETY OF MIND*

▦ **Treading ve-e-e-ery carefully!!**

This chapter is structured differently from the others, because the other party is someone you've been close to all your life, and you're probably going to have to be the more flexible and understanding part of the equation than with other relationships.

Unlike the other chapters in this book, this time you're going to look at the other person's value system before you take another look at yours.

Along the way of our growing up and our parents growing older, two things happen. First, even though we are adults in our own right, often when on home turf (the place where we grew up and where our parents still live) roles get repeated. Dad often dismisses our ideas. Mom treats us as a teenager. Big brother gets bossy. We become whatever our role was in that dynamic.

> *Like actors who find themselves invited only to play the villain or the hero, ordinary people may be continually enlisted to enact certain parts for others.... Very often, people who wish to change find themselves up against the dictates of others' scripts, which seem to insist that they either perform their accustomed role or leave the stage. While we are main characters in our own dramas, we are subordinate players in the dramas of others*
>
> — RUTHELLEN JOSSELSON, JASON ARONSON

We tread on very delicate ground as our parents age, particularly if they have been successful in life and taken care of themselves and others along the way. There *will* come a time, however, when the roles will reverse, and you and your siblings (if there are any) will have to step up, very gently, to start planning for the what if's and when's.

More than 43 million Americans provide care for someone older than 50 who is aging or disabled. Nearly 1 in 10 women ages 45 to 56 is a member of the "sandwich generation," taking care of an aging parent as well as her own children.

Margaret MacAdam, gerontologist, international speaker, researcher and writer on the care of the elderly puts it this way: "It's important for all members of the family—especially children and siblings—to have regular conversations about what's going to happen when, for end of life care."

Here are some guidelines:

- Maintain open communication without ego or "positioning" plays (I'm the oldest so I know best).
- The children need to be clear about what the parents want to happen, and when.
- If the parents are still a couple, they can usually take care of themselves and each other longer.
- Avoid forcing assistance or help on them unless you believe they are really in danger.
- Remember, they have more life experience than you do, and they know what they want.
- Set up opportunities for open communication as a family group. If necessary, include out-of-towners through Skype. This prevents "seagull management" when decisions have to be made. (In Ken Blanchard's *The One Minute Manager*, the term "Seagull Manager" describes individuals who manage by raising alarms based on little knowledge, provide negative feedback, then leave others to clean up the mess. According to Blanchard, "Seagull managers fly

in, make a lot of noise, dump on everyone, and then fly out.")
- Become informed about the options available *before* a crisis. For instance, did you know that in many places you can receive coverage for hospice care? Do you and your sibs know the difference between long-term care, a retirement home, a nursing home, and assisted living?
- Start the conversation early, even though it may be difficult. Remember their value system and work with it. The discussion should include both financial care and personal care. What would they like to happen? And when?

> *Occasionally I've seen children become heavy-handed and insensitive when dealing with their aging parents, and it only caused resentment and hard feelings.*
>
> — BILLY GRAHAM

Research has shown that with most aging parents on the threshold of needing their children's help, they need two things:

- A powerful need to maintain control over their life when age and illness is making it difficult to maintain control.
- Plus the need and desire to appreciate that their life had meaning—they have a legacy of some sort, even grandchildren who love them. And the endless stories they tell, sometimes the same one frequently, is a way of confirming that the life they have lived matters.

Once we understand that, we can learn to soften our approach to "taking charge."

So let's talk about your parents' value systems, remembering that they may differ greatly from yours.

Your Parents' Life Values

My Father's Life Values are:

_____

_____

_____

(e.g., hard work, pride, family, ethnic heritage, and so on.)

My Mother's Life Values are:

_____

_____

_____

(e.g., family, education, keeping face, helping people, and so on.)

Take a thoughtful look at what you believe their values are, put yourself in their head, and imagine how they are feeling around the issues of losing their freedom, their vitality, and their choices. It will help you to be kinder and more understanding when you get push-back. Because you will.

Remember always: do you want to be right, or do you want to be loved? These are difficult times for both the parents and their children as the roles switch, sometimes gently over time and sometimes suddenly in the case of severe illness, accident, or loss.

Life's challenges are not supposed to paralyze you; they're supposed to help you discover who you are.

— BERNICE JOHNSON REAGON

This is the time to find and become your best self. You'll be glad you did. And remember to ask yourself the following questions:

- How do I keep this relationship healthy?
- What did I do today that seemed to improve the relationship?
- Did my actions enhance and enrich the relationship in the long term?
- What are my concerns about this relationship?
- What do I really want from this relationship?

Key Learnings

- Be kind first, then practical.
- Work from their value system, not yours.
- Unless it's a matter of life and death, err on the side of their decisions.
- Listen—truly listen—then decide.

Worksheets For This Chapter

✔ Father's Life Values
✔ Mother's Life Values

CHAPTER 7

You and the In-Laws

Govern a family as you would cook a small fish—very gently.

— CHINESE PROVERB

So you just got married, and now you have another family to deal with, their expectations, traditions, and family problems. Don't assume that your partner's family relationship will be like your own. How you interact with your parents and siblings, inside jokes, old irritations, affectionate teasing, or emotional avoidance may be the total opposite of your growing-up family experience.

I believe we consciously know a part of this, but when reality hits (*Wow! These people are different. They talk over each other at the dining table. They seem to live in each other's pockets.*) while you come from a quiet, reserved, maybe even emotionally distant family. The difference can be quite disconcerting.

> *Often new husbands and wives assume they'll be loved and accepted by in-laws on the merit of having married the in-laws' child. This may be the case, but it usually takes time to establish trust and respect.*
>
> — ROMIE HURLEY

When I first met my mother-in-law I was surprised by how quirky she was. Warm and welcoming, but definitely quirky, unlike her son. I don't know why I assumed (and we all do, I think) that the parents would be a copy or distillation of the person I had partnered with. Not so. Yes, we come from the same soil, but we grow differently. Nature or nurture—either way, we are different from our parents, and sometimes that difference can be dramatic; at other times, not so much.

Expectations play a huge role with in-law relationships, and depending on the parent-child culture, sometimes there's absolutely no wiggle room to make the in-law relationship unique. Sometimes the culture insists that those expectations are cast in stone.

Many families within a South Asian, Middle Eastern, Indian, or Asian culture adhere to well-defined roles and expectations of their children and the children's spouses. (Caveat here: for all those groups with strong in-law expectations I've failed to mention—I apologize!) Before marrying into any one of these cultures, I strongly recommend that you be aware of the expectations and your future role in the family structure. At best, it can be welcoming, loving, and supportive; at worst it can be invasive, bullying, and destructive. To discover expectations, your best plan is to ask another sister/brother-in-law in the same family about what the roles, responsibilities, and expectations are of being the wife or husband of a first-born or youngest member of the family. Do your research, and there won't be any shocks or disappointments on both sides of the relationship.

> *Did you realize that when you married your Prince or Princess*
> *Charming, you inherited the king, the queen, and the whole*
> *court? In a real sense, you did marry the whole family.*
>
> — DR DAVID STOOP AND DR JAN STOOP,
>
> *THE COMPLETE MARRIAGE BOOK*

Even the best in-law relationships take some adjustments, as both sets of in-laws and you come with history. We bring the ghosts of all our past relationships and life experiences with us. We are instinctively sensitive to situations that for others may not even be noticed. And most often, the child of the in-law parents (your partner) doesn't even see or feel what you are experiencing. They grew up with it, and for them it's the norm. Like a fish in water, they don't know it's there until they're taken out of it.

When the relationship is mostly workable and, hopefully, loving and in-clusive—with respect and boundaries observed—take it as a blessing, and never, ever take it for granted! Realize that you have their child in your care, and although everyone here is an adult, the feelings this generates can initially be primal and protective.

"I don't think she realizes she's taken my son away from me," wailed a normally elegant, self-contained, successful physician who had reverted emo-tionally to the state of a mother leaving her first born at daycare! "And he loves her more than he loves me!"

Is this irrational? Yes.

Is it inappropriate? Yes.

Is it common? Yes, but not often a feeling spoken out loud.

My long-time client felt safe enough to allow this feeling to come to the sur-face, even though she knew that in reality it didn't make sense. Her son was 32 and his bride the same age. The relationship between the bride and mother-in-law was a good one. They liked and respected each other, but that didn't stop the feelings my client had in "losing" her first born to another woman.

> *The mother-in-law/daughter-in-law relationship is one of the most complicated human connections. It comes with a built-in conflict before the relationship even begins: two radically dif-ferent views of the same man. One woman always will see him first as a man; the other always will see him first as her child. Understanding these perspectives is the first step to having a smooth in-law connection.*
>
> — ELISABETH GRAHAM

I'm not pointing this out to be overly dramatic, but just to demonstrate how much outside feelings can invade what on the surface looks like a simple relationship. It's worth remembering none of us travels alone. We carry all of our past relationships and experiences with us, so when faced with what seems like an ordinary situation that goes awry, be aware that most often things are more than they appear to be. That's why kindness, courtesy, acceptance, and a positive attitude can oil the wheels of potential conflict or bad feelings. Always remember, they raised your partner to be the person you love and chose to share your life with. So they did something right!

In-Law Appreciation Chart

On days that may be more trying than others, you might want to remind yourself of the good times and the blessings you've been given by your partner's/family:

3 things I appreciate about my mother/father/sister/brother-in-law	3 ways my in-laws contribute positively to my life	3 things my in-laws said or did today/this week that represent their best qualities and strengths
1.	1.	1.
2.	2.	2.
3.	3.	3.

Toxic Relationships

There are times, for whatever reason, that the in-law relationship is so toxic it's almost impossible to have a relationship at all. But for the sake of your partner's relationship with his or her parents, and the hope of your children having grandparents in their life, it's worth the effort to have at least a cordial relationship. Dr. Susan Forward, in her book *Toxic In-Laws,* groups difficult in-laws five ways:

- The Critics who will always tell you what you're doing wrong
- The Controllers who try to run you and your partner's life
- The Engulfers who make never-ending demands on your time and energy
- The Masters of Chaos who live in drama and never-ending problems, and
- The Rejecters who let you know they don't want you as part of their family because you'll never be good enough for their son/daughter.

I wonder what would happen if rather than regarding these folks as having indelible personalities, we considered that, like us, they are capable of being many ways. They may take on the character of disagreeable or critical, but this only works if we allow it to connect in that way.

> *Everything that irritates us about others can lead us to an understanding of ourselves.*
>
> — CARL JUNG

If we can find a way to mentally and emotionally shrug and say, "That's how they are right now. How am I right now? Can I change how I am, because that may change them. And if it doesn't, the very least it will do is help me feel better." We create ourselves and our interaction with each other, usually to emotionally please ourselves, so what I'm suggesting is that with intractable or difficult in-laws, it's worth trying something new—something different.

When we don't take on the other person's drama or attitude, we retain our power. We become the manager of the interaction. If they are snappy or unkind and we are softly spoken and acting out of a spirit of generosity, then we retain our soul self and don't become diminished in any way.

When confronted with what feels like a no-win situation
involving an in-law, use the "drop the rope" theory. Imagine a
rope, the kind used in tug-of-war. If you find yourself provoked,
see that rope in your hands. You can choose to continue yanking
on it —or drop it. Dropping it may sound as though you're
giving in or giving up, but it's actually very empowering. It's
also much more effective than tugging back and forth.

— ROMIE HURLEY

Yes, it's probably not fair that you have to do all the work. We know the world isn't fair, so why get upset about it? Why not just take charge and act the way you want to act, from your highest self. This way, you won't get sucked into the drama. Your partner will respect your understanding of his/her difficult parents, and your kids will learn generosity of spirit in how to deal with difficult people. That in itself is a valuable life lesson you are teaching them.

It's also worth remembering that your partner is torn between their role as their parents' child and your spouse. Finding themselves in the middle of endless bickering between both sides makes your spouse feel disempowered, resentful, and used—not ideal emotions for a loving partner!

To limit confusion and minimize conflicts, it works best if each
of you is the primary spokesperson to your own parents when it
comes to working out differences. Also remember to keep your
relationship with each set of parents separate and positive.

— INGRID LAWRENZ

Life Values And Priorities

To keep yourself and your partner on track through difficult times with the in-laws, work within your Values and Priorities, both short and long term. It might be worthwhile also to look at what your in-laws' value system is. It will help in understanding their motivation and behaviors. This will become the blueprint for your success in future travels through troubled waters with your in-laws.

In-Laws Value System (guessing from what we know)

1. _____

2. _____

3. _____

4. _____

5. _____

6. _____

Their Current Feelings and Priorities (guessing from what we know)

1. _____

2. _____

3. _____

4. _____

5. _____

6. _____

My Relationship Values

1. Kindness
2. Family

3. Health
4. Love
5. Respect
6. etc.
7. etc., etc., etc.

Our Short-Term Priorities – Partner and Kids

1. _____
2. _____
3. _____
4. _____
5. _____
6. _____

Our Long-Term Priorities – Partner and Kids

1. _____
2. _____
3. _____
4. _____
5. _____
6. _____

Love and acceptance goes a long way. We want people to love and accept us the way we are, so let's make sure we do the same: love and accept them the way they are. Be patient with each other. Make time to have fun together, and don't forget to thank them frequently for your beloved partner.

What you say and do now in relation to your in-laws (and parents) will set the tone for years to come. Getting off to a good start is very important because it is difficult to undo the first impression. Go slow and listen more than talk. Different families have different ways to show love, affection, [and] approval.

— STEVE AND KATHY BEIRNE,
PUBLISHERS OF NEWSLETTER FOUNDATIONS

And always remember to ask yourself the following questions:

- How do I keep this relationship healthy?
- What did I do today that seemed to improve the relationship?
- Did my actions enhance and enrich the relationship in the long term?
- What are my concerns about this relationship?
- What do I really want from this relationship?

Key Learnings

- Be aware of any cultural expectations in your new role.
- Kindness goes a long way, as does generosity of spirit.
- Their family dynamic isn't the same as the one you grew up with.
- Long term, it's worth aiming for a workable relationship in which everyone wins.
- Try not to engage in tug-of-war situations that can only escalate. Drop the rope.

Worksheets For This Chapter

✔ In-Law Appreciation Chart
✔ In-Laws Value System
✔ In-Laws Priorities
✔ Your Relationship Values
✔ Your Short-term Priorities
✔ Your Long-term Priorities

SECTION TWO

—

Friends, Lovers,
And The Unloved Ones

CHAPTER 8

You and Your Ex

A heart can stop beating for a while; one can still live.

— SUZANNE FINNAMORE, *SPLIT: A MEMOIR OF DIVORCE*

Whether you've spent two or 20 years with your ex, separating is rarely easy or pleasant. Someone is the "dump-er" and the other person is the "dump-ee." The dump-er is often filled with guilt and a fear of losing the kids (if they have any). The dump-ee is hurt, bewildered, embarrassed, and angry. No wonder the chances of having an "adult" conversation about this are knife-edge slim. And that's when there's been no abuse or infidelity. Imagine what it's like when you add in these two volcanic situations!

Another complicated relationship. So much of an "ex situation" depends on how you exited from the relationship (hence "ex"), the timing, and who else is involved, such as children, beloved in-laws, mutual friends, and even co-workers.

The reality is that everyone's ex situation is different, and some people's recovery rate is faster than others. The goal here is to act with grace and dignity, respecting your boundaries and his or hers, allowing you both to move forward out of the relationship into a life of peace and to separate one from the other as far as circumstances allow. This should be a learning in your life, not a destruction. So let's plan to make it work *for* you, not against you. And maybe, possibly, one day, you'll be able to interact with your ex with a smile and kindness, and no lasting "ickyness."

You spent time together, you loved each other, and now you've separated. Allow yourself to grieve, because you are in mourning. If you can, recruit a support system from a nonjudgmental circle of friends or a professional therapist; in order to heal and move on, there is no question you are going to need help. And by the way, that help should not come from your ex—it's over, it's finished, it's gone. On the other hand, if your ex calls, emails, or stops by your house, seeking comfort for his or her broken heart, kindly and firmly let them know that you're no longer his or her support system. Shut the door and move on.

> *Now, it is natural to "get" very upset and agitated when things aren't going as you would like. But is natural necessarily always good for you? No! It most assuredly does feel good—temporarily— to get things off your chest, but that rarely helps solve problems that won't go away (just because you blew up), and indeed it often makes them worse. An alternative is not to hold these feelings inside, but rather to attack them and reduce them to a level that enables you to handle the situation more functionally.*
> — ALBERT ELLIS, PH.D. & ARTHUR LANGE, ED.D.

Ben came to see me because he had split from his wife and she wasn't letting him see his two children, a boy of eight and a girl of 12. He missed them both so badly that it had affected his work as a sales rep for a large technology company, and had to take time off to, as he put it, "deal with my depression." They hadn't started legal proceedings, because he hadn't known what to do. He had been in a turmoil ("like my brain has turned off") since he was thrown out of his house when his wife, Sheila, found he'd had sex with a colleague while at a recent convention.

"It was just one time; we both had too much to drink. It didn't mean anything! I'm not sure if this is permanent or she's just blowing off steam," he explained. "But she won't let me near the house. She put a bag of my clothes outside the garage and told me to pick them up before it rains."

Eventually—and I mean eventually, like toward the end of the session—he admitted that this had happened before. When he'd had too much to drink he would have sex outside of his marriage.

"So this is a pattern," I said.

"Yes, but it never means anything," he told me.

"It obviously does to your wife," I said, and he agreed with that.

I gave him the homework forms to make the relationship contract, first with himself and then, hopefully in the not-too-distant future, with his wife. He agreed he had to know and understand what was really important for him in a relationship and why he used alcohol as his "one foot out the door" when he had the opportunity to do so. He agreed that he hadn't been happy in the marriage for a while, but he didn't know what to do about it.

Before he came back for his next appointment, Ben had to connect with his wife and ask if she would also consider working on their relationship possibilities with the Third Circle Protocol. In addition to the Values, Priorities, Needs, Wants, and Gives, he was to look at which two human needs he was currently fulfilling, and if he thought they gave him what he wanted/needed. We booked a two-hour session for the following week.

I gave Ben this sheet, along with the Third Circle Protocol package.

The Six Human Needs

Choose your top two:

- Certainty
- Variety
- Significance
- Love and Connection
- Growth
- Contribution

How do your needs serve you currently in your view of your world? Look at your old story and move into your new story ("We can do this together").

Use blame to move forward—bad blame and good blame ("We can do this together").

Both Ben and his wife, after writing their Third Circle Contracts, realized their relationship was over. With no blaming, they parted reasonably amicably, with the children shared and all the legals handled smoothly by a media-tor lawyer. Both Ben and Sheila moved forward, knowing themselves better and what their next intimate relationship would look and feel like: what they needed, wanted, and were prepared to give.

Warning!!

After a breakup, if you're the one who is left behind, it's only natural to feel abandoned, angry, sometimes resentful and bitter. It's all too easy to go on-line—whether texting or Facebook or some other form of networking site—and spew your anger, disappointment, and frustration to others. Don't do it! Resist the temptation, or you'll regret it in the future.

> *We know the world is not fair, yet we still get overly upset when it's unfair to us.*
>
> — ALBERT ELLIS & ARTHUR LANGE

Do This Instead

This may be the time when you need to remember how successful or valuable you've been in other situations or for other people. Just close your eyes and remember a time when you brought all your wisdom, kindness, and maybe humor into a situation for a friend or colleague, and that the help you gave them made them feel stronger and more motivated to move forward. Now, as you remember this, with your eyes still closed, gently rub your finger and thumb together, locking in that ability you have to use your wisdom and kindness to feel better—only this time, it's for you! The more you do this the stronger it becomes, and knowing that you have the wisdom and kindness within gives you even more strength to move forward. Repeat this exercise at least twice a day so that your body and emotions react automatically into a place of peace when you need it. This protocol works brilliantly if you train yourself and practice regularly.

Unless you live in a cave or another country, the chances are you're going to run into your ex somehow, somewhere. So plan for it. Imagine the absolute worst-case scenario, e.g., you're looking awful, in grungy jeans and your hair is a mess; you've just popped out to the corner store for milk, and your ex is there with the most perfect-looking person… Chances are that that's not going to happen. Your ex encounter will probably be more mundane, in the supermarket or at a party or even on the street. However, the pain and the longing may still be there. It will certainly trigger some sort of feeling, whether it be anger, lust, or just plain loneliness. But remember, what's done is done. Your ex is now your ex. Hold your head high, and move on as gracefully as possible.

The best rule of thumb to get over an ex is to avoid all contact if you can for at least six months, and use that time to better yourself, to grow and flourish; maybe plan a well-deserved vacation, train for a marathon, something, anything, that will help you heal and move on.

However, if you have children, that's not so easy to do. This is where reevaluating your values and priorities becomes key.

If you find that your ex makes everything into a drama and it's defeating your plan of learning to be self-sufficient and without trauma, there are a few things you can do:

- You can ignore all emotional content in texts and visits and relate only to the relevant issue, using a few words in a neutral business-like tone. Yes, I know, it's easier said than done, but it will give you a wonderful sense of control and self-management.
- Also, you don't have to answer the phone, and you don't have to respond to every text, particularly if it's a rant or a nasty message.
- We are very easily caught in emotion around issues to do with our children or other loved ones, so it's important to learn to ignore petty communications.
- When you're replying to something that triggers you in some way, wait at least an hour before sending the response. Center yourself (learn how to at the end of this chapter); only after you come down and feel calm and collected should you respond. Make that response as neutral as possible and make sure you stick to the facts.

- Understand that separation or divorce is rough and you're going to get pulled into old patterns every so often, so give yourself a break. Take a deep breath, and use the exercise at the end of this chapter to help you get through this each time it happens.

> *The only thing more unthinkable than leaving was staying; the only thing more impossible than staying was leaving. I didn't want to destroy anything or anybody. I just wanted to slip quietly out the back door, without causing any fuss or conse-quences, and then not stop running until I reached Greenland.*
>
> — ELIZABETH GILBERT,
> *EAT, PRAY, LOVE*

By understanding the buttons that are being pushed by your ex, you will come to learn that we all have three main buttons and that if you respond immediately, one of yours has been pushed. If you can ask yourself, *Which button did he/she just push?*, you will have moved from reaction to thoughtful action. You will have moved from emotion into considered thinking, and that gives you back your power. So, here are the three buttons that most people have:

- I'm not good enough (as a parent, a partner, a person).
- I'm stupid.
- I'm irrelevant (my thoughts and feelings don't matter).

> *No one can make you feel inferior without your consent.*
>
> — ELEANOR ROOSEVELT

As a clinical counselor for the past 20 years, I can tell you that most people, at all levels of life, have these three shiny, waiting-to-be-pressed buttons. So step back from the trigger comment or text, check which button it pushed, and think about this: The comment is really not about you or the current situation; it has more to do with the fact that your ex-partner knows where you're vulnerable and knows which button to push. Tell yourself: *Not anymore!* You now know what to do:

- Look at it
- Acknowledge it, and
- Let it go.

… in spite of the possible feelings of hurt, anger, betrayal, sadness, and loss you may be carrying. You are going to manage your emotions by acknowledging them as yours and not letting your ex trigger them.

Values And Priorities

During this time, it's valuable and constructive to review your life values and your priorities. These priorities will depend on the next steps you need to take, the people involved, and the legal and financial issues—because, ultimately, your ex did share a piece of your life and you don't want the relationship or the ending of it to damage the rest of your life. You're going to manage the relationship so that it becomes, at worst, benign and, at best, a good memory. Agreed?

> *A 2011 study published in the Journal of Applied Social Psychology showed that the more one's self-worth depends on a relationship, the more suffering one is likely to feel when it's over.*
>
> — LISA A. PHILIPS

So, let's look at your priorities over the next six months, and combine these with your set of values, to give you a plan of action and a way of behaving that allows you to be in control and manage your emotions and life better.

I suggest you take a sheet of paper and write down your six or eight key life values and then, on another sheet of paper, write down your priorities for the next six to 12 months. These priorities might include such things as ease of handling the children's visits to your ex, or dealing with the issue of your ex dating, or finding a way of downsizing your home so that you can manage it alone. Line up the two lists so they look something like this:

Values	Priorities
Family	Peaceful interaction with kids
Healthy living	Activities with kids
Respect	Careful, considered communicating
Kindness	Don't speak badly about ex
Friends	Laugh and have fun with friends
Good work ethic	Take courses for a career

If you partner these Priorities alongside your Values, you can then set goals for how you're going to manage the next six months with your head held high, demonstrating to your children that, by respecting your ex, it's okay for them to love their other parent. If you do this, you'll find that your life becomes kinder to you and your kids won't feel guilty about wanting to be with their other parent. Plus you learn to manage all interactions much more easily.

> *The divorce has lasted way longer than the marriage, but finally it's over. Enough about that. The point is that for a long time, the fact that I was divorced was the most important thing about me. And now it's not.*
>
> — NORA EPHRON

Exercise For Relaxing And De-Stressing

As I mentioned earlier, there will be times when you will need to center yourself, relax, and find a place where you don't feel hurt, angry, or dismissed. This exercise, which I suggest you record on your MP3 player or computer, is a brief relaxation or self-hypnosis script that you can use at any time—*but not while you're driving your car!* Speak it slowly and gently into your recorder, and use it anytime you feel stressed. It can even help you sleep better!

Find a quiet spot where you won't be disturbed and, if you can, put your feet up, legs uncrossed, hands separate. Take a deep breath, and as you exhale, close your eyes, and begin to follow your breathing. Notice the coolness of the in-breath and the warmth of your out-breath ... just notice how evenly and smoothly your breath flows, gently flowing in and out.

The coolness of the in-breath and the warmth of the out-breath. Nothing bothers you. Nothing disturbs you. Nobody wanting anything, nobody needing anything, this time is for you. Just follow your breath while counting from 1 to 20, with each third out-breath taking you deeper into relaxation—1, 2, 3, 4, 5, 6 ... deeper relaxed ... 7, 8, 9 10, 11, 12 ... deeper down ... 13, 14, 15, 16, 17, 18, 19, 20 ... relaxing down ... deeply.

On your next out-breath, imagine a large ball of golden light about 12 inches above your head, and whether you see it or imagine you see it, it doesn't matter. This ball of light will slowly emit rays of relaxation through your body, in tune with your breath, and it will feel like a warm, gentle releasing of all tension, thoughts, and negative emotions.

Allow it to happen now ... feel the golden light touching the top of your head, moving down your face and the back of your head, releasing all the muscles in your face, your jaw, your neck, the back of your shoulders, the front of your shoulders ... down, down, into your chest, through your back, down your spine, vertebra by vertebra, relaxing down ... from your shoulders now ... down into your arms, into your hands, and the light travels to the end of your fingertips, relaxing your arms and hands so they feel heavy and relaxed

… moving the light now, down from your chest and all the muscles around your ribs, relaxing … let the light move into your stomach, your hips, into your upper legs, your lower legs, and your feet. Right down to the ends of your toes… Your whole body relaxing into this beautiful golden light.

Allow yourself to drift and float in this light.Allow it to heal and nurture you—mind, body, and soul. Allow the light to heal any emotional or physical pain, and give grateful thanks for your inner strength. And allow the compassion and unconditional love of the universe to flow through you now… As you feel the gentle healing of the light, stay here as long as you wish, and when you are ready to return to your daily world, count slowly and gently, back … 10, 9, 8, 7, 6, 5, 4, 3, 2, and 1. Rejuvenated, relaxed, and in control.

Welcome back.

Key Learnings

- Expect to be in grief for a while. Move through it thoughtfully and gracefully.
- Make a plan for the next six months using Values and Priorities. Set goals.
- Find a support team, and use them as support, not a crutch.
- Give yourself six months to heal and rebuild.

Worksheets For This Chapter

✔ Human Needs
✔ Life Values
✔ Priorities
✔ Exercise for Relaxing

CHAPTER 9

You and Your Date

You come to love not by finding the perfect person, but by seeing an imperfect person perfectly.

— SAM KEEN, *BABY BOOMER AUTHOR AND LECTURER*

At its best, dating is an experiment that can be fun; at its worst, it's a dismal letdown. Like all experiments, we can learn from failures. What went wrong? Did we set expectations too high? What did you discover from your last two or three dates that you can put into the learnings for the next two or three? Yes, successful dating is usually a numbers game. The smart way to think about dating is to consider it a learning process for mind, body, and spirit. It's a bit like learning to run a marathon. First you walk, then you jog, then you run 5k, then you run 10k, and then you run the marathon. Slowly does it.

In its purest form, dating is auditioning for mating (and auditioning means we may or may not get the part).

— JOY BROWNE, *DATING FOR DUMMIES*

Another way to think of it is that it's like a wine tasting. Different vintages, different flavors—all are good, but not everyone is to your taste. And that's okay, too!

Yeah, But Why Do I Always Get It Wrong?

- How come I always choose losers?
- How come they all look so good in the beginning and then they change?

- He/she seemed so caring in the beginning, then it became suffocating.
- I like strong, self-sustaining women, but the last one left me feeling unnecessary; she was too self-sustaining!
- I'm such a giving person. All the women I meet, I end up taking care of, then they leave me.
- Why can't I find someone to take care of me for a change?

We are what we repeatedly do.

— ARISTOTLE

If you're one of those people who keeps repeating the same mistakes when looking for a lover or a mate, you should know you're in a rut. It's a conundrum, because we can't change something if we don't know a) that it's our pattern (everyone initially shows up looking so different) and b) how we stop doing that!

Let's take a look at some of the possible patterns you find yourself in. Are you:

- Frightened to ask what you want to know for fear of losing the connection: ("Are you … married? in a relationship? seeing someone else?")

- Choosing people who:

  - are not close to or talking to their families;
  - seem to be married to their job rather than the people in their life, always working late, or traveling out of town more than staying in it;
  - would rather spend their evenings with the boys (or girls) than at home with you;
  - seem caring, but quickly become possessive and abusive;

– have the negative aspects of your father; or
– have the negative aspects of your mother.

I know we're talking about dating, but let's also consider what we hope dating can lead to: falling in love; because you don't want to fall in love with someone who is:

– mean to you;
– not fun to be with;
– always controlling;
– not inclined to be monogamous;
– wants to be "joined at the hip," doing everything together;
– shows signs of jealousy;
– drinks too much;
– uses illegal substances;
– is moody and sulks;
– puts everything and everyone else before you (i.e., job and buddies).

We need to be aware of what not to ignore. Yes, some of these may seem obvious but, trust me, it happens. I'm not sure if people think they can change their partners or just choose to ignore the obvious. Don't!

That's the not-so-good news. Now for the good news!

You're dating as a grown-up! If you're smart, you'll dispense with the game playing—the mind reading, the jealousy or hard-to-get game—and get real right from the get-go. That doesn't mean you tell all on the first date; it just means, be who you are. Really.

Dating is about finding out who you are and who others are. If you show up in a masquerade outfit, neither is going to happen.

— HENRY CLOUD,
HOW TO GET A DATE WORTH KEEPING

Trudy is a 32-year-old lawyer—chic, energetic, with a smile to light up the room. She came to see me because she didn't understand why the men she chose to date bored her or disappointed her in some important way a few months into each relationship. We talked about the four stages of most dating relationships and decided to investigate together at which stage hers always broke down.

- Infatuation/Romance stage
- What the Heck Happened? stage
- Dealing with the Differences stage
- Fight-or-Flight stage
- Commitment and Co-Creation stage

I asked her about the infatuation stage for her. What did she look for in a date-with-potential?

She wanted intelligence, someone who is a self-starter, ambitious "like me," someone who is focused and excited about life. Not a guy who sits in front of the TV and watches sports all the time. She also said she liked slim, good-looking men who were a bit taller than her ("not too much, just a bit"). I noticed, but didn't say anything, that she hadn't included kind, loving, family values, humor, or respect.

Trudy said that it was always exciting, with great sex and anticipation at the beginning, and sometimes that feeling lasted "even as long as two years—my longest relationship."

"My two-year relationship with Ralph was really good at the start. We had so much in common; we were even born within a few days of each other! Not the same year, but the same month. How crazy is that?!" They traveled a lot together, sometimes piggy-backing on his business trips when she could get away. They took a wine course together, took out a joint membership to the museum so they could attend the lectures together, and started a nonfiction book club with some of their mutual friends. And they were talking about moving in together.

Everything seemed fine at the first level of the relationship. So, what happened in the next level? Is this where it breaks down?

"Sounds perfect," I said. "What happened?"

"I started noticing how he wasn't always there for me. Sometimes he'd cancel a date at the last minute, saying he had to work late. Or when I was sick, he didn't come over because he didn't want to catch my cold or flu, saying he had an important contract to complete and couldn't afford to get sick." Trudy also complained that the sex wasn't as exciting. It became routine. "Even the flowers he brought for me every Friday were the same flowers," she said accusingly.

The second level is where most relationships start to fray around the edges. It's then that we start to notice irritating habits as the "frisson" of the new chemistry between us starts to simmer down and our beloved ain't so magically marvelous anymore. Instead of seeing similarities, we start noticing the differences and our partner's flaws. Irritability often sets in (*How come they changed on me?* or *They hid that part of themselves from me. How can I trust them now?*) Often at this time, one partner draws away and the other becomes clingier, wondering, *What the heck happened?*

"I'm always the one that pulls away," Trudy commented. "Somehow I always feel betrayed, like there's a lie between us."

Trudy had become a serial dater, always taking the exit the minute it "didn't feel right." She never allowed herself to experience the "Stability Stage," where the couple learns to discuss their differences and allows the other person to be who they are: different yet respectful of each other and their differences. She didn't deal with level 3 at all: "Fight or Flight"; she just flew! Trudy never allowed herself to move onto the "Commitment" stage of planning a future together, even though she said that was what she wanted.

After this discussion—an eye-opener for Trudy—we decided we needed to plan a series of clinic appointments that would help her discover:

a) who she really is, underneath the mantle of "lawyer";
b) what she really wants in a life partner—if she truly wants a
   long-term relationship at all!;

c) when and what caused her to be so protective of her vulnerability that she couldn't allow herself to be emotionally intimate and available—whether it was a childhood issue, or something about her professional persona that didn't allow her to relax.

Of course, there was homework. I gave her what I'm giving you below. If Trudy's story seems familiar to you, go for it and do your homework!

Who Are You?

Let's find out. Answer these simple questions (that are not so simple), and you'll have more idea of who and how you are. That way you'll know more about what you're looking for in a date and a mate.

WHO am I?

(Sample answer: I am male/female [age]. I am a daughter, mother, son, father, friend, and I have a career/job as a _____ , which I find satisfying, etc., etc., etc.)

Who AM I?

(Sample answer: My spirit is connected through my awareness of [religion, spirituality, meditation, etc., etc.] my highest self, and through this I know that I AM.)

Who am I?

(Sample answer: I am joy in the springtime, playing hockey with the guys, celebrating my part in family, surrounding myself with music and nature, etc.)

My Life Values are:

1. _____

2. _____

3. _____

4. _____

5. _____

6. _____

7. _____

8. _____

The five things I need in my life to feel loved are:

1. _____

2. _____

3. _____

4. _____

5. _____

Now you know who you are—maybe even discovering pieces of you that you didn't know existed before!—we can talk about the date and what type of person you're looking for (leaving Johnny Depp out of this—remember, you're an adult now <<grin>>). What you need to consider is the combination of body type, personality, mind, and spirit; how the person relates to you; the way you laugh, interact, listen, talk, and touch together.

> *Sexiness wears thin after a while and beauty fades, but to be married to a man who makes you laugh every day, ah, now that is a treat.*
>
> — JOANNE WOODWARD

Needs – Wants – Gives

So what do you really *need* from any person you date? (Example: Respect. Monogamy. Good conversation. Likes the arts. Likes animals, etc.)

1. _____

2. _____

3. _____

4. _____

5. _____

What do you *want* from any person you date? (Example: Slim, healthy body. Humor. Likes to "do" things. Likes his/her family, good sex, etc.)

1. _____

2. _____

3. _____

4. _____

5. _____

What are you prepared to *give* your date? (Example: Fun, monogamy after third date, interested in lots of things, like to travel, pay own way, etc.)

1. _____

2. _____

3. _____

4. _____

5. _____

Dating is supposed to be fun. The minute it becomes tense or troublesome, this person isn't for you. Move on. And when it is fun ... also move on, and become a couple. But that's another book.

> *A healthy relationship promotes self-growth. If you think that being with someone makes you a better person, you're tapped into the idea of personal expansion.*
>
> — ARTHUR ARON *OF SUNY STONY BROOK*

However, if you are moving on, it doesn't hurt to ask yourself the following questions:

- How do I keep this relationship healthy?
- What did I do today that seemed to improve the relationship?
- Did my actions enhance and enrich the relationship in the long term?
- What are my concerns about this relationship?
- What do I really want from this relationship?

Key Learnings

- Dating is rehearsing for the real thing.
- Be real, otherwise you're just kidding yourself and the other person.
- Be clear about your needs and wants in that order. Never ignore the need.
- Remember to have fun!

Worksheets For This Chapter

✔ Who am I?
✔ Life Values
✔ Needs – Wants – Gives

CHAPTER 10

You and Your Friends

Friendship is always a sweet responsibility,
never an opportunity.

— KHALIL GIBRAN

Do you ever find yourself wondering, *What happened to...?* as you think about a friend you had when you were younger, maybe in high school or even kindergarten? People we care for passionately as friends—particularly those friendships of our youth—have a sad way of slowly melting away from our day-to-day lives.

We do change over time. We change, and so do our friends. Sometimes we grow out of our friendships; sometimes we grow closer. Life happens, and friendships often change with life circumstances, and it takes work to stay in touch with old friends through distance, life-altering events, and plain busyness. But sometimes we just have to let old friends go. They were great through college and maybe during dating times, but the reality is that when you move forward in life, you may need to change your friends. Some people aren't interested in seeing you grow and improve. Your values and priorities change. Your sense of adventure or need to keep learning takes you into new pathways, and your old friends don't always like the changes you're making, or your new points of view. Your new interests don't match theirs, and so you just have to move on.

But also, we change, and the people we are interested in become different, and we understand that no one person can be everything to us. Every friend offers something special. One may be great for movies and parties, another may share our love of sports or hiking, and another may be the friend we can talk to about our deepest feelings.

I don't need a friend who changes when I change and who nods when I nod; my shadow does that much better.

— PLUTARCH

So let's check in and see how our Values and Priorities may have changed over the past 20 years or more. (Yes, I know, I'm assuming you're over 30!)

Life Values And Priorities

My Key Life Values today are:

1. _____
2. _____
3. _____
4. _____
5. _____

My Key Priorities are:

1. _____
2. _____
3. _____
4. _____
5. _____

Current Limitations in my life are: (*e.g. time, no car, etc.*)

1. _____
2. _____

3. _____

4. _____

5. _____

6. _____

When I was younger I wanted my friend to:

- Be easily available (at school or next door, etc.)
- Be fun to laugh and giggle with
- Play "pretend" with me
- Talk about our dreams
- And... (you add to the list here).

Now I want a friend to be:

- kind
- a good listener
- available to do things with
- fun
- (you add to the list here)

...and notice the difference.

The false notion that a friend is a friend forever, no matter what, has caused much heartache. All relationships experience ups and downs, and it is important to overlook occasional misunderstandings and differences of opinion. However, if a relationship brings you more pain than pleasure, it is time to reconsider whether or not it is a true friendship, and one that should endure.

> *No person is your friend who demands your silence, or denies your right to grow.*
>
> — ALICE WALKER

Long-time friendships are valuable. They represent the familiar, the warm, the comfort of an old shoe—they fit, are a little worn away through rough times, but still there and still sturdy. Never, ever, take them for granted. They need to be polished, nurtured, and given time, or made time for—yes, time set aside—to honor and respect what you have both been through together. They are the golden threads in our tapestry of life—of people coming and going, life changes; they are the solid, reliable touchstones of our human-ness. Use your calendar to make sure they are kept in the circle of your life on a regular basis. Not always easy, but valuable—in all ways.

Making New Friends

Some of your old friendships may have survived the transition through the years, but if most of them haven't, then what?

As we get older, it's not always easy to make friends, but here are some ideas that can help you bridge that gap between the familiar and the new.

Remember that making friends as an adult is different. *Know yourself. Chase your passions, not people.*

> *Don't walk behind me; I may not lead. Don't walk in front of me; I may not follow. Just walk beside me and be my friend.*
>
> — ALBERT CAMUS

Not everyone we meet is going to want to hang out with us. And definitely not everyone we hang out with is going to become a close friend. We're just not compatible with most people in terms of interests, values, what they're looking for in a friendship, availability, and a dozen other things. So while you can try to apply the following ideas to your new friends, realize they're not all going to go the distance and become your soul mates. That's okay though, since you may still be able to enjoy their company on a more casual level.

For friendships to form and be maintained, you need consistency. As a kid, this was automatic. You went to school, summer camp, and played with other kids in the neighborhood. As adults, we rarely have that kind of consistency

117

outside of work. There are exceptions, of course. And I suggest you consider one or more of the following ideas if you want the opportunity to make new friends.

Join groups that meet on a regular basis, such as associations, networking groups, book clubs, classes, and workshops. Groups build consistency; people show up just because. There's usually one or two people that you would like to develop a friendship with. This is the time to take these people—or that person—out of the "container" of the group. Suggest a movie or coffee time; suggest an opportunity to have fun and do something else together that's interesting. If you don't build on that opportunity, and the people you connect with inside that container aren't seen outside the container, the relationship will most likely fade away when the group activity or class ends.

Sometimes we'll become good friends with someone pretty quickly; at other times it takes a while.

> *Friendship is born at that moment when one person says to another: "What! You too? I thought I was the only one."*
>
> — C.S. LEWIS

Overall, if you're making an effort to become better friends with someone, and you get the sense you're putting more energy into it than they are, consider backing off and adjusting your expectations. Finding good friendships when you're beyond baby-bearing and university years can be a little like chasing the elusive white whale. You know it's possible, but it takes focus, dedication, and commitment.

We are creatures who thrive in community. Research has shown that we live longer, healthier lives with friends and community around us. It may take effort, but it's important. Give the act of connecting with others the time and space it deserves – and you deserve!

This is also a good time to consider volunteering. No, don't groan! Yes, you do have the time. Even one morning a week. You'll meet new people all focused on the same thing. The food bank. The hospital. The community theater. The youth drop-in center. In addition, you may want to check to see if there is a volunteer recruitment center in your area. There often is. They all need whatever time and energy you can consistently give.

> *The language of friendship is not words but meanings.*
> — HENRY DAVID THOREAU

And, keeping in mind that in friendships, the relationship is the "Third Circle," remember to ask yourself the following questions:

- How do I keep this relationship healthy?
- What did I do today that seemed to improve the relationship?
- Did my actions enhance and enrich the relationship in the long term?
- What are my concerns about this relationship?
- What do I really want from this relationship?

Key Learnings

- Keeping friendships alive takes time.
- Not every friendship lasts through a lifetime.
- Make time for fun and shared experiences in friendships.
- Look for new people to join your community of friends. Consistency is the key to building and maintaining friendships.
- Be kind.

Worksheets For This Chapter

✓ Life Values
✓ Priorities
✓ Limitations
✓ Wants

CHAPTER 11

You and the Unloved Ones

Let us not look back in anger, nor forward in fear, but around in awareness.

— JAMES THURBER

This chapter is about the people you are supposed to like or love but can't stand, such as extended family or friends of friends. Currently, most relationships are forged from the erroneous idea that we have to be the same to get along and that differences between us are to be avoided at all costs.

We all have 'em. Friends that we love deeply who have friends we can't stand. Extended family members who are disruptive, emotionally diminishing, or just plain pains in the butt! If we had the choice, these people wouldn't be a part of our lives but because they are, through loving connections with others, we have to find a way of making the relationship with them work (without too many sighs or feelings of martyrdom, which are soooo unattractive <<grin>>).

Often in our minds, conflict can be resolved only with an I-win-you-lose self-righteous stance (legs spread, hands on hips, chin raised!). But that doesn't work long term in any setting. And if your unloved ones are going to be with you for a while (a job, a family, or a friend of a friend), you need to rethink that and really grow up. Put your big person pants on, and make it work.

Living alongside our "unloved ones" takes some planning, forethought, and initial work. We need to go inside ourselves to find out what *exactly* bothers us—and then realize that we expect people to take us the way we are, but we don't take other folks the way they are! It's a shocking truth, but it's reality. So if we don't first take the time to go within ourselves, we often go without the peace and freedom that comes with understanding and allowance. We also need to recognize all the "yes, but's" we put up along the way.

It isn't the mountain ahead that wears you out; it's the grain of sand in your shoe.

— ROBERT W. SERVICE

So let's start. In general, we usually like people who are like us: same values, same patterns, same way of seeing the world. So if we can find a way to make ourselves in some way—however small—like or appreciate the person who drives us crazy, there's a possibility that we can make our life easier.

"You are kidding, right? Make myself like that idiot who drives me nuts. Madame Drama Queen? Gossip-hungry, two-faced know-it-all. Why would I want to do that?"

Relax… I'm not asking you to turn into a mealy-mouthed, small-minded person, or a world's-coming-to-an-end drama debutante, or even a gossip-hungry, smiley-faced, stab-you-in-the-back cousin. Listen carefully, and read s-l-o-w-l-y (yes, calm down…). I said, make ourselves, in some way—*some* way, which includes subconscious body movements, speech patterns, even breath rhythm. Because science has shown that human beings all have a need to be accepted and appreciated. We subconsciously check for similarities or differences in others. We need to find—or make— a "sameness": the existence of common ground, of common humanity. If we can make ourselves similar by something as simple as breathing in the same sequence, or talking at the same pace, or sitting in the same position, we create a deep subconscious feeling of acceptance. And the other person doesn't even know it's happening. In neurolinguistic programming (NLP) jargon, it's called "rapport"—subconscious rapport. All the other person knows is that they feel more comfortable with you. You might want to read some NLP books or take some classes to find out more. I promise you, it will make a h-u-u-u-ge difference in your life, especially in your relationships with the unloved ones.

Generosity arises on its own steam. It is not debated. It comes without being bidden. It comes because your heart simply desires to go this way and not another. Your heart may not even

be aware of feeling generous, because this is what your heart
wants to do, the same way you open a window when you want
a breeze.

— HEAVENLETTERS.ORG

The next level of change in moving toward co-habitation on this planet with the unloved ones is listening. Really listening. Listen to the other with a view to understanding, not disagreement or agreement. This is not the time to prove you are right and they are wrong. You are listening and learning their view of their world so that you can better understand their personal needs, hopes, dreams, and wishes. Whether or not they share the same political views or social understandings as you do, it's more important to realize where you are similar—love of family, animals, the outdoors … whatever. Make it your goal to find the sameness, not the differences. It changes the energy between you. Everyone wants to be accepted and respected for who they are. It's your job, as the person who wants to live in harmony, to find that place in them that can be respected and accepted in your mind and heart. Be generous with yourself, without losing your core. Life gets easier that way. And most importantly, you retain your power – your strength. You don't lose it to anger or irritation. You are in charge!

The willingness to accept responsibility for one's own life is the
source from which self-respect springs.

— JOAN DIDION

Life Values Changes Chart

List and look at your life values, and see how you can apply them to this relationship. Never mind what you perceive the other person to be—Untrustworthy, Mean-Spirited, and so forth—it's what *you* are that will make the difference. And if one of your values is Kindness, then use it, knowing that how you change will change the relationship and the energy around it. Once you change the energy, everything changes.

Life Values:

1. _____

2. _____

3. _____

4. _____

5. _____

How I might use these to change
the relationship with (*name*)_____

1. _____

2. _____

3. _____

4. _____

5. _____

When this happens _____

and I feel _____

I will take a deep breath, remembering my values and commitment to
harmony, peace, and empowerment, and I will respond this way:

_____

Knowing how you respond to any situation is the first step to change. We
can't change anything until we know what we're changing. And change takes
time, in addition to awareness. How we respond to others is a pattern, a

habit, stemming from old responses. Habits and patterns take time to change, but the awareness is a *must, first.*

Here goes! Ask yourself:

- How am I inappropriately feeling and acting in this situation?
- What's going through my head, and what am I feeling in my body to respond this way? Irritable? Self-righteous? Fearful? Resentful?
- About myself
- About the others
- About the situation?

What can I realistically substitute for my awful-izing, should-ing, and rationalizing? How about:

- I want …
- I'd like …
- I'd prefer …
- It would be better if…
- What feelings would result if?…
- It's unfortunate…
- I'm disappointed…
- I'm seriously concerned…
- I regret…
- I'm committed to…

And remember, once again, to ask yourself the following questions:

- How do I keep this relationship healthy (or as healthy as it can be for the sake of my best friend, family, co-workers, and so forth)?
- What did I do today that seemed to improve the relationship?
- Did my actions enhance and enrich the relationship in the long term?

- What are my concerns about this relationship?
- What do I really want from this relationship?

Key Learnings

- Living in anger or irritation is no way to live; it's damaging to mind and body.
- There are always some points of connection if we look hard enough.
- They are who they are, and they have a right to be who they are … as do you.

Worksheets For This Chapter

✓ Life Values Changes Chart

SECTION THREE

—

The Business Connection

CHAPTER 12

You and the People You Pay —
The Professionals in Your Life

You hit home runs not by chance but by preparation.

— ROGER MARIS

This chapter deals with the professionals in your life. This includes your lawyer, your hairdresser, your physician, your therapist, your fitness trainer, your financial planner, your insurance broker, your dentist, your coach, your massage therapist/chiropractor/naturopath, and so on. When choosing someone whose services you will be paying for, be aware of your value system and what you *need, want,* and will *give* to this relationship.

Work It Through

- I absolutely NEED from my (lawyer, therapist, etc.)

  _____

  _____

  (e.g., confidentiality, at least five years' experience, a familiarity with my type of issues, etc.)

- I WANT (or would prefer)

  _____

  _____

  (e.g., someone who is on time, who is pleasant to be around, who I feel enjoys what they do.)

- I will GIVE

  _____

  _____

  (e.g., preparation and homework completed for each appointment, pay my bills on time, etc.)

For the other side of the coin, I interviewed a wide range of professionals who become our "help circle" in life to find out from them what makes a good client/patient relationship. Interestingly, they all came up with the same basic six answers:

1. Pay your bill on time.
2. Come to the meetings/sessions prepared.
3. Time = money, so use it wisely.
4. Be honest; don't play games with our professional relationship.
5. If you cancel with less than 24 hours' notice, be prepared to pay at least part of the fee.
6. I'm not your friend.

1. Pay your bill on time.

This shouldn't need any explanation, but it seems it does. And the more friendly the relationship, the more difficult it becomes to discuss overdue invoices and payments. Many professionals, for that reason alone, have learned to keep their clients at arm's length. "Friendly, collegial but not too personal" is how one family court lawyer explained it to me.

A personal trainer told me about one of her clients who kept putting off paying, month after month. At the third month, when she was told the sessions couldn't continue without payment, the client said hotly, "But I thought you were my friend!"

2. Come to the session prepared.

Being prepared is, of course, different for each professional. Here are some examples of being professional with your professional!

LAWYER

For the first meeting, it can be a huge timewaster for you and your lawyer if you don't come to the meeting prepared. It will end up costing you a lot more money.

- Bring notes (two copies: one for you and one for them) succinctly explaining what you want them to do. Include the brief (and I mean brief) history of the circumstances—just the facts: dates, names, actions—*not* your feelings, or your belief about what the other people are thinking, or your mother's, brother's, friends' feelings and opinions. You're paying this professional by the hour. They want the chronological facts, the history, key players, where you are right now with the issue. Also include in these notes, all your personal information, full name, address, email, phone number, and so on.

- Any documentation you have that applies to the issue, make copies and bring them. It's not good enough to talk about the documentation or emails and tell them that you have them "somewhere at home, I think."

- Take notes during the discussion, because you'll be keeping your own files.

- Talk fees, payment plan, what by when. Tell the lawyer what you want them to achieve. Be honest.

- Talk next steps, dates and actions– yours and theirs. And make a note. You want to be very clear before you leave the office. Every subsequent phone call you make because you don't remember, or didn't understand, will cost you!!

DOCTOR
- If it's a new doctor, come with medical records and your list of medications and treatments.
- Come with notes about the issue—the more specific the better.
- Take notes of what the doctor is saying, including medications, timing, and so on. If it's something very serious or possibly life threatening, take someone with you to make notes, because you'll be too emotionally upset to remember exactly what was said or to ask relevant questions.
- Some doctors take the time to develop a conversation and a collegial atmosphere in the meeting, which is good to have. But not all doctors do that. Don't take it personally; just make sure you get what you need from the visit.
- Dress casually if you are expecting a medical examination— you don't want to have to struggle with shoes or clothing when disrobing or getting dressed again.

MASSAGE THERAPIST/FITNESS TRAINER
/CHIROPRACTOR
- Be prepared to discuss some medical issues with them.
- Come with goals in mind, and let them know, specifically, what you expect from them.
- Discuss fees, timing, and projected outcomes.

DENTIST
Be considerate. Come with clean teeth! You'd think that would be obvious, but unfortunately it's not.
- Discuss program of treatment and fees.
- Dress for possible water splashes!

THERAPIST
- Bring brief notes about the issues you wish to cover. These notes

should include your name and contact information.

- Document briefly your life history: where and when you were born, key relationships and dates. Include your physician's name and contact info, plus any current medications.
- Be honest at all times. Nothing will shock your therapist— they are professionals and are not there to judge you. And they've probably heard it all before!

5. Cancellations

Life happens, and sometimes you just can't make your appointment. Most professionals have a 24-hour cancellation policy. In other words, if you call, text, or email the morning of, or late the night before, you will be charged for your appointment. Your professional is in business, and they sell their expertise by the hour. If you cancel too late for them to fill that spot, they have a right to charge you for it. Of course there are emergency exceptions, and if you're a long-time client, your practitioner may waive the fee.

We've just covered points **2**, **3**, **4**, and **5** in the examples above. Now let's talk about point 6.

6. I'm Not Your Friend

Anyone you pay for their time and expertise is a professional working on your behalf to achieve the best for you, in their own way. You are a client, a customer, a patient; you are *not* their friend.

> *It's embarrassing when a client starts talking about her personal issues. I know she feels familiar with me because I'm handling her body, but I'm not a therapist, or a friend. I'm working on her for an hour to help her body heal. I have to be friendly, so she feels safe, but that's it.*
>
> — **RMT** *(REGISTERED MASSAGE THERAPIST)*
> *WHO KEEPS HER CLIENTS FOR YEARS.*

Yes, part of our job is to make our clients feel good, so they can get through the workout parts they dislike, so sometimes I flirt a little, or laugh at their jokes, or sympathize about their wife or husband's issues, but really, I'm just the hired help!

— PERSONAL TRAINER.

It's so disrespectful when a client says, 'While I'm here, can you just have a look at this contract my sister is supposed to sign for her new job?' Or, 'While I'm here, can you tell me what I should do about making sure my dad keeps me in his will?'

— A FAMILY LAWYER

When I asked the lawyer how she handles this, she laughed and said mostly she just says, "Would you say to your physician, 'While I'm here, can you tell me what my sister should do about her indigestion?' Then I explain, 'It's really not my area of expertise.' I make a semi-joke about it and hope they get the point."

Bottom line, it doesn't matter how long you have worked with this person, and how friendly they are—lawyer, trainer, doctor, hairdresser, therapist—when you stop paying them, they won't be there. They are not your friend.

Before you book your next appointment, think about Dr. Phil's "Seven Steps to Acquiring Your Goals":

- Express your goal in terms of specific events or behaviors.
- Express your goal in terms that can be measured.
- Assign a timeline to your goal.
- Choose a goal that you can control.
- Plan and program a strategy that will get you to your goal.
- Define your goal in terms of steps.
- Create accountability for your progress toward your goal.

And, once again, this is a relationship, so it wouldn't hurt to ask yourself the following questions:

- How do I keep this relationship healthy?
- What did I do today that seemed to improve the relationship?
- Did my actions enhance and enrich the relationship in the long term?
- What are my concerns about this relationship?
- What do I really want from this relationship?

Key Learnings

- For all professional "help," time is money.
- Come prepared for your time with them.
- Treat them with respect, be on time, and if you have to cancel, give 24 hours' notice.
- If you have a complaint, tell them directly so the issue can be fixed.
- Do they have the same integrity and work ethic as you (or a better one)?
- Gossip doesn't belong in the treatment room.
- They are not your friend!

Worksheets For This Chapter

✓ Needs – Wants – Gives

CHAPTER 13

You and Your Boss
... Or Why Are You Staying
in This Job?

Without ambition one starts nothing.
Without work one finishes nothing.
The prize will not be sent to you.
You have to win it.

— RALPH WALDO EMERSON

To win in the marketplace you must first win in the workplace.

— DOUG CONANT

When I was in the corporate world during the time I didn't own my own business, I had to learn to put up with bosses who were a) rude, b) uncomfortable with senior women managers, and c) continually finding ways to dismiss and diminish my personal values and accomplishments.

And yet the pluses of staying in the job far outweighed the negatives. At least until they didn't!

The most senior guy in the company would set up meetings with me to discuss a client issue and then would answer his phone every time it rang, or start reading some correspondence on his desk (before computers, which isn't *that* long ago), while making really helpful comments like "sounds like a plan" or "hmm, that's not going to be easy to sort out, but find a way" or "I'm leaving for Europe, so I can't help you." And, by the way, this was in a service business!

One day, I went to him to help resolve a client crisis. It was important because the client was due in the office within the hour and expected to meet with him as well as myself to help him solve the problem. He, the boss, needed to be prepared. I walked the length of the room to sit opposite him at his desk, carrying a briefing sheet for him and me, and as I did, his phone rang. I said, "Please don't pick it up. This is time-sensitive. Mary will let you know if it's urgent."

He stood up, leaned across the desk until his face was three inches away from mine, and yelled, "How dare you tell me what to do." He sat back down, picked up his phone, and proceeded to talk to someone—obviously not a client.

I went back to my office, shaking, and knew I had to get myself together for the meeting and somehow do it without him. I was thinking about who else I could strategically bring into the meeting with me so that we could help the client solve their crisis without the "figurehead" being there.

A few minutes later, I had arranged the team and was preparing my notes, still shaky but focused. The big boss came to my office, closed the door behind him, and said, "Did you want to speak to me?" I replied, "Not anymore." He turned and walked out of my office, slamming the door.

The meeting went well, fortunately. That evening, I was packing up to go home and my boss came into my office and said, "I think I owe you an apology."

"Yes, you do," I said. "Don't ever speak to me again like that. I don't deserve it, and you should know better."

Quiet for a moment, he said, "I apologize," and left the office. I felt drained, but knew I had done the right thing.

Often, I've counseled executives who had no idea just how intimidating or disrespectful they were when speaking to employees. When in a panic, they tended to respond with aggressive speech meant to frighten others into changing their behavior in order to placate upper management. This approach shuts down productive communication, reducing the manager's ability to see the larger picture, make better decisions, and effectively influence his or her team.

Always treat your employees exactly as you want them to treat your best customers.

— STEPHEN R. COVEY

My regional boss was in Chicago, and for most of the time acted like I didn't exist—even when I was in the room. During regional senior exec meetings (managers from North and South America), he would turn sideways when I went into his office for a pre-presentation meeting. (Note: Bosses like to know what you're going to say before presenting your report at a major meeting. They don't like surprises, either about year-end numbers or projections.) I'd walk in, say, "Hi, Alex," and he'd mumble, "Hi," and turn sideways. After a while, I found it amusing.

Also, at the cocktail party after the major meetings were over and we could all supposedly relax, I would go up to him, drink in hand (single malt Scotch then!) and say something simple like, "Alex, how are the kids?" He'd step back two steps and mumble something. Undaunted, I'd move forward to try to connect with him at some level. He'd step back. After a while I realized that having a polite one-on-one conversation with him was like doing the cha-cha. I'd step forward, he'd step back, I'd step back, he'd step forward … cha cha cha.

Yes, it was childish, I know, but it was the only way I could find to keep from screaming "IDIOT!" at him: by amusing myself while not diminishing him.

We learn many different ways to achieve each kind of goal.

— MARVIN MINSKY

My DM (Deny-Me) manager, was what I used to call the guy in New York who never admitted to a good idea that came from the office I managed—although many of them were implemented internationally—and who was always sarcastic about my personal community involvements for the company. Even though we always met or exceeded bottom line projections, neither I nor my team ever got acknowledgment for it. Of course, I recognize that no one does a good job alone; there is always a team, and ours worked together really well and was respected by our international colleagues. But while I was leader of the team, we didn't get the credit that was due to us, purely because I was female. Our success was always made light of, and I felt not considered important enough to acknowledge with the same sort of kudos other offices received. But I stayed because at the time it was worth it. I was learning valuable tools and meeting extraordinary people, both from the client side and the creative side. Some of them are still in touch, many years and career iterations later. Plus, of course, the salary was really, really good.

> *No yesterdays are ever wasted for those who give themselves to today.*
>
> — BRENDAN FRANCIS

So why am I telling you this? Because first, you must have a good relationship with yourself (see Chapter 2). If you have a good relationship with yourself, you can make any situation work—as long as it works for you, and as long as you keep learning, and your priorities and values are mostly met. And second, because there is also a need to come to terms with what a relationship with your boss is really about. And what it is not.

Obviously, the following points won't apply to every job and employee and employer relationship, but there will be some areas where you will get an "aha!"

Your employer is not your parent. They are not there to:

- take care of you
- know about your personal life
- take care of your ego or promote you when you think you deserve it
- be concerned about you not meeting your living expenses, or
- be your caretaker.

Your employer's first priority is to:

- keep their business profitable
- keep their business competitive
- find the best people for the jobs to do the above, and
- keep their boss—or board of directors—happy and looking good.

And it's your job to help them to achieve their priorities. That's what you're getting paid for.

You Are Your Own Boss, ULTIMATELY

Yes, you work for a company, and you have at least one boss, and yes, they, to some degree have influence over your job, your career, and your work life while you're their employee. BUT—and it's a huge but…

If you know who you are, and know your values, priorities, and needs and wants from any relationship, you will see how this job position works for you, and for how long.

So let's start from the beginning with your Values, thinking about how they apply to your working/professional life.

Values

Without a strong relationship and understanding of self, it's virtually impossible to have a strong and deep, lasting relationship with others—any sort of relationship. We have to know who we are before we know what we want/need/can offer in a relationship with another person.

List your key six or eight Life Values and be honest. These are the bedrock values of where you stand in life – what is truly important to you. Maybe you have only four or six key values, but list them in any order.

1. _____

2. _____

3. _____

4. _____

5. _____

6. _____

7. _____

8. _____

Priorities

(Rank in order of importance to you)

☐ ACHIEVEMENT to accomplish a major goal in life, to reach a peak event or performance

☐ AFFLUENCE to amass quantities of money or property

☐ AUTHORITY to possess the position and power to control persons and events

☐ ENJOYMENT to lead a happy life filled with joy and comfort

☐ EXPERTISE to attain skills and knowledge in many areas

☐ FAME to become prominent, well known, famous

☐ FAMILY to belong to and contribute to a close family relationship

☐ FREEDOM to possess freedom of thought and action

☐ FRIENDSHIP to belong, to be liked, to be accepted and admired by others as a friend

☐ **INFLUENCE** to influence people and events through the force of personality and ability.

☐ **LOVE** to give and receive warmth and understanding, to be involved in close, affectionate relationships.

☐ **RESPONSIBILITY** to honor and accomplish certain fundamental responsibilities.

☐ **SECURITY** to obtain a safe, stable, and secure place in life.

☐ **SELF-ACTUALIZATION** to strive to and attain the limits of personal and professional development.

☐ **SERVICE** to help others attain their goals, to serve and support purpose that supersedes personal desires.

☐ **SPIRITUALITY** to feel that what I'm doing is not just of my own making but is part of something that belongs to a larger creation.

YOUR Needs, Wants, and Gives

- What is in the contract—usually unrecognized until too late—of your ideal career relationship?
- What do you *need* that's non-negotiable?
- What do you *want* that's preferable?
- What are you prepared to *give* to your career relationships?

SWOT Analysis

With this next exercise, you'll be able to work out your value to the workplace—your "brand," if you like. Because ultimately we are all CEO's of our own career, our future in the job market. The good news about this is that once you understand it, and the principles behind it, you have a chance to stand out, to be promoted, to get a better, more interesting, higher paid job. With your bosses' help, or without it.

So what makes you different? What helps you make a positive impact with your boss, and your boss's boss? Let's find out what you add to the company that is remarkable and where you add value, both to the brand of yourself and to the company.

This is called the SWOT Analysis (SWOT stands for Strengths, Weaknesses, Opportunities, Threats). You may have done it before somewhere or sometime, but now you're doing it with a different focus. Spend some quiet time doing this. It's worth it.

SWOT
(Strengths, Weaknesses, Opportunities, Threats)

Here are some suggested categories for analysis:

Strengths

- Education
- Work ethic
- Transferable skills
- Personality attributes
- Work experience
- Character
- Training ability
- Community profile, etc.
- Add others here

Weaknesses

- Weak planning or execution abilities
- Lack of focus
- Low energy
- Little relevant experience
- Weak detail or big picture focus
- Lack of ability to prioritize
- Lack of time management skills
- Add others

Opportunities

- Self-growth
- Networking
- Building bottom line from X to XX in first, second, and third year
- New markets
- Training programs
- Inter-company exchange program
- Add others

Threats

- Growth of competition
- Management changes
- Slow business
- Office disruptions
- Add others

Now that you've done the analysis, what does it mean? It adds another level to your self-knowledge and self-awareness—what you can and currently do not, bring to your job.

You And Your Boss – Revisited

Now that you've done these exercises, you have more understanding of yourself and what you bring to your job, and you will find it easier to go to your boss with concerns or questions.

Before emailing or connecting with your boss to sort through an issue, make a commitment to yourself to remember that his or her reaction to you isn't about you. It's about them—what they are dealing with in their life. They too report to someone; even an owner-operator reports to the bank! Their personal issues can include insecurity, lack of management skills, fear of losing their job, or they may just be a control freak or bully. Once you understand that part of the dynamic, nothing they say can really affect you at a deep level; you recognize what's going on and don't let it affect you. Don't let it turn into a battle of egos, or a "he said–she said" exchange.

> *The challenge of leadership is to be strong but not rude; be kind but not weak; be bold but not a bully; be humble but not timid; be proud but not arrogant; have humor but without folly.*
>
> — JIM ROHN

Plan for a discussion rather than a confrontation, using a win-win strategy focused on goals, problem solving, and asking for advice. In other words, *you need to manage your manager!* And if you remember that you are the CEO of your own brand, then this job, the current position you hold, is there as long as it works for you and your career. *You* are in charge here (but don't tell the boss that!).

And *always* ask yourself the following questions (because this is, after all, a key relationship in your life—one that affects your well-being on a daily basis):

- How do I keep this relationship healthy?
- What did I do today that seemed to improve the relationship?
- Did my actions enhance and enrich the relationship in the long term?

- What are my concerns about this relationship?
- What do I really want from this relationship?
- Is there something I need to do right away to correct it?
- If not right away, when?

Key Learnings

- Your boss is not responsible for your growth or happiness on the job; you are.
- Always find one or two solutions before you present a problem.
- Know your values and stick to them—until they don't work for you, then re-calculate and re-evaluate.
- Your job is to help keep the company effective and profitable and your boss successful.
- Know when it's your time to move up or on and redo your goals and plan for that move.

Worksheets For This Chapter

✔ Values
✔ Priorities
✔ Needs – Wants – Gives
✔ SWOT Analysis

CHAPTER 14

You and Your Employees

If you want to build a ship, don't drum up the men to gather
wood, divide the work, and give orders. Instead, teach them to
yearn for the vast and endless sea.

— ANTOINE DE SAINT-EXUPÉRY

Becoming a boss for the first time can be a huge wake-up call—whether as an entrepreneur who has hired their first one or two people to work in your company, or if you've been promoted and you're now the boss of the crew you partied with a few weeks ago!

You're about to find out that being a boss is not the same as being an employee. Being a successful boss, a manager, a leader is both an art and science. There's the ever-important interpersonal skills (the EQ) and the science of successfully managing, mentoring, and measuring the tasks with the employee.

Employees who believe that management is concerned about
them as a whole person— not just an employee— are more
productive, more satisfied, more fulfilled. Satisfied employees
mean satisfied customers, which leads to profitability.

— ANNE MULCAHY, *FORMER XEROX CEO*

Being a boss involves looking at the work, the team, and the company from a different perspective. The boss has a different focus and different tasks to accomplish. The focus and work of a boss are more long term in outcome, more on target for the company's bottom line.

So even when you fully understand what your employees do, you may not always be able to make decisions that your employees feel are in their best interest. This can cause discontented mutterings from your former party crew! The "folk ethic" demands that we behave in an egalitarian manner, which is fine. Unfortunately, it spills over into confusion when it says, "We are all the same." Not true. As long as you are paying people as employees, you're not the same as them!

> *Connect the dots between individual roles and the goals of the organization. When people see that connection, they get a lot of energy out of work. They feel the importance, dignity, and meaning in their job.*
>
> — KEN BLANCHARD, *MANAGEMENT EXPERT*

Let's talk about the two different ways of "being a boss." You're the entrepreneur, and it's your company. You're the owner of a small business—in command of your own destiny, calling the shots, forging new strategies, managing personnel, and making key business decisions on a daily basis. Or you've been promoted, or just hired in, and you're managing a group of people—some you may have known before as equal colleagues, or they're new to you, and you to them, and they're watching you to see what new ideas you're going to foist on them that they know won't work.

Everything changes when you're in charge. Instead of following directions, you must generate them. Instead of focusing on your job, you focus on the company. Instead of worrying about your annual bonus, you worry about being able to afford bonuses, and who deserves how much. Being in charge also means wearing many hats, such as operator, accountant, visionary, and heavy. This collection of millinery skills has generated plenty of schools, talks, discussions, and articles with a name all its own: Management. So it's time to upgrade your view of your business self: the who you are and how you are in the business world you inhabit—owner-operator or just-promoted senior manager.

Either way, we first need to visit your value system and priorities. Before you start claiming that "this soft stuff doesn't belong in business," let me remind you that we take ourselves everywhere we go. So go for it!

Life Values

My eight key Life Values are:

1. _____

2. _____

3. _____

4. _____

5. _____

6. _____

7. _____

8. _____

Priorities

(Rank in order of importance to you)

- [ ] ACHIEVEMENT to accomplish a major goal in life, to reach a peak event or performance

- [ ] AFFLUENCE to amass quantities of money or property

- [ ] AUTHORITY to possess the position and power to control persons and events

- [ ] ENJOYMENT to lead a happy life filled with joy and comfort

- [ ] EXPERTISE to attain skills and knowledge in many areas

- [ ] FAME to become prominent, well known, famous

- [ ] **FAMILY** to belong to and contribute to a close family relationship

- [ ] **FREEDOM** to possess freedom of thought and action

- [ ] **FRIENDSHIP** to belong, to be liked, to be accepted and admired by others as a friend

- [ ] **INFLUENCE** to influence people and events through the force of personality and ability.

- [ ] **LOVE** to give and receive warmth and understanding, to be involved in close, affectionate relationships.

- [ ] **RESPONSIBILITY** to honor and accomplish certain fundamental responsibilities.

- [ ] **SECURITY** to obtain a safe, stable, and secure place in life.

- [ ] **SELF-ACTUALIZATION** to strive to and attain the limits of personal and professional development.

- [ ] **SERVICE** to help others attain their goals, to serve and support purpose that supersedes personal desires.

- [ ] **SPIRITUALITY** To feel that what I'm doing is not just of my own making but is part of something that belongs to a larger creation.

Swot Analysis

Let's evaluate what you bring to the roll of boss by doing your SWOT analysis. After this, you may find you need more training in some areas, or the use of a business coach for six months or so. Or you may find you have talents and knowledge you haven't recognized or been given the freedom to use before.

The key to success with SWOT is to make sure you answer honestly, not from the ego or "wish-I-was" part of you, but from the reality of who you truly are. The good, the bad, and the downright ugly! Remember, this is for your eyes only, and if you do this correctly, you will find areas to celebrate and areas that need work. If you do the work, you will be successful beyond your wildest dreams. If you don't, you could turn out to be the boss from hell, and that always, always affects the bottom line.

> *Success at the highest level comes down to one question: "Can you make the choice that your happiness can come from someone else's success?" No one has qualities like courage, vision, charisma, adaptability, and decisiveness in equal measure. But every great leader does make the same decision— and so can you.*
>
> — JEFF HADEN

Swot Analysis Worksheet

Strengths

- What do I do well?
- What unique resources can I draw on?
- What do others see as my strengths?

Weaknesses

- What could I improve?
- Where do I have fewer resources than others?
- What do others see as my potential weaknesses?

Opportunities

- What opportunities are now open and possible to me?
- What trends could I take advantage of?
- How can I turn my strengths into opportunities?

Threat

- What could prevent me moving forward?
- What is my competition doing? (inside and outside the company)
- What threats do my weaknesses expose me to?

Moving Forward

- What are the next three actions I need to take for success?
- By when?

Okay, that's the art; now let's look at the science.

Whether as an owner-operator or newly minted manager, one significant question to ask your employees— "What's the least useful thing you're working on right now?"—demonstrates to your employees that their opinions count, and that their time is valuable. When you have the right people working together and feeling heard, you begin to see the benefits of a widespread sense of shared ownership.

Because the challenges facing a small business owner are somewhat different from a member of a large organization, I have split the rest of this chapter into two parts. But there are learnings from both sections that will apply to both of you.

> *If you are a boss, you should know as much about the people under you as you can. What do they want? What are their goals? What are they trying to accomplish? Not what you want. What they want. You know what you want. The key is what they want and how you can help them achieve those goals.*
>
> — RICK PITINO

PART ONE
You've Been Promoted to Be the New Manager

If you've become "the boss" through promotion in your existing company, establishing new relationships with your former colleagues will not be the only challenge you face. You also will need to discard your junior image and redefine yourself to the company. Don't assume you know what is expected of you. Take the time to learn what your superiors and your internal customers want from you with regard to:

- the *strategy* – If it's right, it doesn't take much wall clock time; if it isn't right for now, maybe that's why you've been promoted, making your new priority the new strategy;
- the *culture* – As a boss, it's your job to reinforce and maintain the corporate culture, motivating, elevating, and selecting and promoting from within your new team; and
- whether, in your new role, you will be involved with an *additional focus* such as distribution, product development, or sales. Be very clear what your new role includes, as well as the expectations around it.

Staying in the same corporation but in a different role brings its own challenges.

1. You'll have to make decisions people won't like. Whether it's ending a popular incentive program, not hiring an employee's friend, or telling your team that they need to work late, managers have to make decisions that their teams aren't always happy about.
2. You'll have to tell people when they're not doing a good job. Sometimes these are people you like and people who are genuinely trying hard. These conversations are difficult, and many managers hate them, but they're also unavoidable.

3. Unfortunately, you'll need to give up some workplace friendships. Since managers need to have professional boundaries between them and the people they manage, you can't have the same types of office friendships that you had before you became a manager. You might really click with someone on your staff, but you can't become close in the same way you could before—particularly if you're in the same division or section of the company.

4. Don't assume that your existing relationships with colleagues will continue as before. Some of them who also aspired to the position may be jealous. Former pals may no longer welcome you to their social gatherings. A resentful few may even try to sabotage you.

5. Now it's time for you to have a new set of alliances with other senior managers whose ranks you have joined. Communication and cooperation with these new colleagues is key to success in any corporate environment.

6. Some people just won't like you. If you're doing your job, not everyone is going to like you. You are going to tell some people their work isn't good enough; hold accountable people who may not want to be held accountable; enforce policies that may irritate the heck out of some people; and yes, fire people. It's unnerving to know that some people will dislike you simply because you're doing your job, but it's unavoidable.

You manage things; you lead people.
— REAR ADMIRAL GRACE HOPPER

Good managers, whether in a corporate environment or a small owner/operator business, are able to straddle the fine line between micromanaging and neglect. One way I've found to make this work is to monitor the employees' work product rather than your employees. Don't allow an employee to get away with bad results simply because she's at work on time and often brings you cookies!

Remembering the results of your Values exercise, bring your values into the workplace. Here are some tips that can help you become a good manager and maintain a productive relationship with your employees:

1. Say "thank you" when deserved, and mean it. Remember, your team has the ability to make you look good or bad. Keep them motivated by recognizing a job well done. Because it's such a simple gesture, it's easy to forget the power this endearing term wields.
2. Keep the lines of communication open. Since it's impossible to be everywhere at once, your staff should know that they can come to you before an issue becomes a major problem. You are the person they depend on for guidance.
3. Accept responsibility for those who report to you. When you refer to one of your staff members (or worse, your entire team) in a derogatory manner when speaking with your superiors, it casts your leadership abilities in a bad light. After all, the competency of those who report to you is a direct reflection of how you're doing your job.
4. Never ask a staff member to do something you aren't willing to do yourself.

A good leader is a person who takes a little more than his share of the blame and a little less than his share of the credit.

— JOHN MAXWELL

PART TWO
The Entrepreneur – The Innovator – The Starter

All owner-operator business owners have a drive to succeed. They are self-starters, rushing to the finish line even when there isn't one! Most have had very little or no business or management training and are learning on the job. And I speak from experience. Because of this, they often run into problems with staff as their company grows. The first one or two employees become close and often a friendship starts, which is a minefield waiting to explode. Roles change as companies grow, and whether a family member or friend, the person in charge of distribution when the bottom line is $20,000 is unlikely to be effective when that figure changes to $200,000 or $2 million.

I have worked with many start-up owner-operator companies, and I always suggest that the whole team do the Third Circle exercise—Values, Priorities, Needs, Wants, Gives—and that each write their contract in partnership with the owner.

As the company grows, and new people are added, roles will change, so it needs to be done again, specifically with the original group of people. That way, they are able to see how they fit into the new paradigm—if at all. By the way, this is equally effective if the company is beginning to fail and someone has to be let go. This first group of people, the nucleus, is often made up of friends, family members, or friends of friends, and is prime material for combustion when things change.

The Third Circle protocol has proved its worth over and over again in these circumstances. People know where they are and what they can give and get from their role in the small business. No false hopes are built up, no pretending there's nothing wrong with the job they're doing. It makes things a lot simpler for the owner of the business to make changes.

> *You'll attract the employees you need if you can explain why your mission is compelling: not why it's important in general, but why you're doing something important that no one else is going to get done.*
>
> — PETER THIEL, *CO-FOUNDER OF PAYPAL*

Most entrepreneurial companies have very little structure to start with. It's only when you get into the third layer of employee that you'll notice you need the structure of a company protocol, a vision and values statement, and job descriptions. If you've been working with your values system all along, and kept everyone in tune with their own business priorities, the growth will evolve more smoothly from an employee's point of view and your bottom line won't be impacted by a revolution of change.

With most entrepreneurs, communication becomes a problem once you hit the third layer of employees. As it was explained to me by The Center for Creative Leadership, entrepreneurs often think and talk at a speed and comprehension of 1-50-100-150-200, whereas most people talk and comprehend at 1-5-7.5-5-6-7-8-9-15-14-16-17-20, and so on, needing to take in the information slower and sometimes going back over the information. This absolutely does not mean that the faster thinker is smarter—not by any means; it just means they process differently from their listener. This is why communication breaks down and small business owners are often perceived as difficult to deal with: they don't understand that the way they are communicating isn't connecting. But that's not you … is it?

When I'm called in to help a client like that, I'm often reminded of the situation that happens frequently when English-speaking people travel abroad and find that they are not understood: they speak louder. It would be funny if it wasn't so rude! I explain to them that communication is just that. You can be talking all you want, but if it's not being received, then you're not communicating—and it's your fault! You need to communicate with your employees where *they* are at—not where you are—if you want the best results for your company.

Regular employee evaluations are key, as is understanding their view of their world, i.e., their values and priorities. If you don't make time for these in your schedule, your business and your bottom line will suffer. Although you're the driver of your business, without your employees on your side you won't be able to service your customers and grow your business. If you don't care about them, they won't care about your business.

Engaged employees are in the game for the sake of the game;
they believe in the cause of the organization.

— PAUL MARCIANO, PHD

To foster productive relationships with your employees, ask yourself the following questions:

- How do I keep this/these relationship[s] healthy?
- What did I do today that seemed to improve the relationship[s]?
- Did my actions enhance and enrich the relationship[s] in the long term?
- What are my concerns about this/these relationship[s]?
- What do I really want from this/these relationship[s]?

Key learnings

- Values and Priorities are key to all leadership roles in business.
- Relationships change, but that doesn't mean they don't matter.
No one succeeds alone; good relationships make the difference.
Meet and communicate to your employees where *they* are, not where you are.
- Regular check-ups and check-ins are important.

Worksheets For This Chapter

✔ Life Values
✔ Priorities
✔ SWOT Analysis

Summing Up

Change is like a house: you can't build it from the top down, only from the bottom up.

— GLORIA STEINEM

Ultimately, we are creatures of community. We thrive when we are part of a healthy "whole" community, when we are fully whole and at one with our self and able to connect with others without judgment or "shoulds." Our happiness is developed when we are comfortable with who we are and allow others to be who they are, too.

It's the realization that when you're an adult no one gets to judge you, and when you're an adult you don't have to defend yourself! You've learned the three buttons, the unspoken contract of The Third Circle, and you've decided to grow up, be whole, generous, and joyous in this lifetime.

It's not what name others call us that matters, but what name we respond to that determines who we are.

— EPICTETUS, *AD 55-135*

Bottom line, you've learned different ways of looking at relationships with yourself and others. Here's one more view: The structure of relationships has four corners, or rooms if you prefer.

- *Be interested* – and you become interesting.
- *Be generous* – There's lots of you to go around—mind, body and spirit!
- *Be involved* – Join the parade of life; don't just watch it pass by.

- *Be aware of your impact* – Every word, touch, action has impact and creates change.

Relationships aren't about finding the right personalities but about creating the right environment in which to flourish. It's not about how much respect and regard you have in the beginning but how much you build until the end.

One Last Exercise – What Needs Work?

As you finish reading this book for the first time—because I do want you to keep coming back, checking in on the chapters that relate to your life situation, and do the work—here is one last exercise:

What Is Working for Me Currently, and What Still Needs Attention?

I am grateful that these relationships are now working well for me	These pieces of my life need attention
1.	1.
2.	2.
3.	3.
4.	4.
5.	5.
6.	6.

Let your "pieces" that need attention become your goals for the forthcoming months.

Mind: What will you achieve by when?
Body: What will you have done by when?
Spirituality: How will you be behaving by when?
Relationship hiccups: What will be different by when?

If you need help, I'm always available through my website, email, or phone. Meanwhile, you are the author of your life. Go write the book!

Addenda And Worksheets

The following worksheets are also available as a separate PDF and can be downloaded at: *http://georginacannon.com/worksheets*

The Seven Questions

To keep to the goal of a successful relationship, ask yourself the following questions:

1. How do I keep this relationship healthy?

2. What did I do today that seemed to improve the relationship?

3. Did my actions enhance and enrich the relationship for the long term?

4. What are my concerns today about this relationship?

5. Is there something I need to do right away to correct it?

6. If not right away, when?

7. What do I really want from this relationship?

Life Values

List your key six or eight Life Values. Be honest; no point in pretending here. Maybe you have only four or six key values. List them in any order.

My eight key Life Values are:

1. _____

2. _____

3. _____

4. _____

5. _____

6. _____

7. _____

8. _____

Priorities

(Rank in order of importance to you and you can change the wording in each category if it's a better fit for you)

☐ ACHIEVEMENT to accomplish a major goal in life, to reach a peak event or performance

☐ AFFLUENCE to amass quantities of money or property

☐ AUTHORITY to possess the position and power to control persons and events

☐ ENJOYMENT to lead a happy life filled with joy and comfort

☐ EXPERTISE to attain skills and knowledge in many areas

☐ FAME to become prominent, well known, famous

☐ FAMILY to belong to and contribute to a close family relationship

☐ FREEDOM to possess freedom of thought and action

☐ FRIENDSHIP to belong, to be liked, to be accepted and admired by others as a friend

☐ INFLUENCE to influence people and events through the force of personality and ability.

☐ LOVE to give and receive warmth and understanding, to be involved in close, affectionate relationships.

☐ **RESPONSIBILITY** to honor and accomplish certain fundamental responsibilities.

☐ **SECURITY** to obtain a safe, stable, and secure place in life.

☐ **SELF-ACTUALIZATION** to strive to and attain the limits of personal and professional development.

☐ **SERVICE** to help others attain their goals, to serve and support purpose that supersedes personal desires.

☐ **SPIRITUALITY** to feel that what I'm doing is not just of my own making but is part of something that belongs to a larger creation.

Knowing Your Own Truths
What Are They?

List three things your teachers told you that you believe but may not necessarily be true.

1. _____
2. _____
3. _____

List three things your parents told you that you believe but may not necessarily be true.

1. _____
2. _____
3. _____

List three things society tells you that you believe but may not necessarily be true.

1. _____
2. _____
3. _____

Write down three of your own beliefs that you have developed that may not be true.

1. _____

2. _____

3. _____

Are these beliefs:

- Out of date?
- Invasive?
- Relevant to you today?

Action Chart

For each category of your life, list the top four or five actions that you think you need to take to improve your relationship with yourself.

	Personal	Family	Career	Spiritual
1.				
2.				
3.				
4.				
5.				

Wheel Of Life Balance

How satisfied are you in each area of your life? See the center of the wheel as 0 and the outer edge as 10 and draw a straight or curved line to create a new outer edge. Write the number you assign to each section i.e. Health & Fitness may rank 7 out of 10. Career may be 3 out of 10. Where you draw your lines is the new perimeter of your Wheel of Life Balance as you see it today.

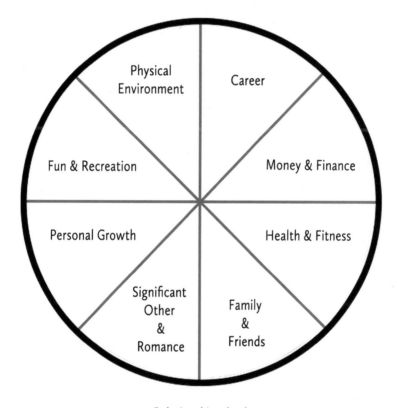

Relationship wheel

Look to see where the scores are low. Check them against the other information you've received from the previous Priorities and Values charts and see what aha's you get! So, for example, if you gave Personal Growth a score of 3, yet listed Self-Actualization (to strive and attain the limits of personal and professional development) as one of your priorities and Being a Good Person as one of your values, then you haven't thought it through and you need to re-evaluate what you mean by "Being a Good Person."

Aha! 1. _____

Aha! 2. _____

Aha! 3. _____

Vision and Goal Clarification Protocol

What do you really, *really* want in your life right now? Here's a way to find out when you're not sure.

1. Get clear on the situation at hand

You need context before you can decide what you want (one thing at a time, please). Is this about:

- Work?
- A relationship?
- Self-actualization?

2. Imagine fantastic, outrageous success

Go on, amp it up. See it clearly, brighten the picture, hear the applause you get from achieving your goal, feel how it feels to be successful … and double that feeling.

What would total and fabulous success look like? Don't get caught up in the "How would I get there?" dilemma. Just focus on what outrageous success looks like—for you.

3. Clarify your minimum level of success

This process helps you reach for the stars. This allows you realistic stations along the way toward your ultimate goal. This is the bottom line, the "if nothing else, then at least this."

Make sure the bottom line really is just that. This is the very least that is acceptable to you.

4. Close your eyes and go inside your imaginative space

Find the sweet spot of what you want, what feels good between those two end points.

Sit with it for just a moment and imagine as clearly as possible what it is you want, what it looks like, feels like, tastes like. Then in your mind and body, double the feeling or visual.

5. Lock it in – any way that works for you

It may be a single word like "okay" or a signal like "thumbs up."

Siblings Dynamic

(Explain in detail under each heading, Physical, Emotional, and Intellectual)

When I was...	My relationship with my brother/sister was...		
	Physical	Emotional	Intellectual
Under 10.			
A teenager			
In my 20s			
And now			
I recognize these old patterns and want to change to this . . .			
In the future			
So that my relationship with my sibling(s) looks and feels like this . . .			
From now on			

Needs – Wants – Gives

The next step toward consciously shaping the relationship is for both parties to answer the following questions:

- What do I **need** from my relationship? *Absolute must haves.*

- What do I **want** from my relationship? *It would be nice to have this in our relationship.*

- What am I prepared to **give** to the relationship?
  What am I prepared to commit to give to the relationship?

This shows areas where each of you is together on your vision of moving forward and where there may be differences.

Forgiveness Ritual

Do the work separately, but come together to complete the ritual.

STEP 1: Complete these three sentences

The thoughts, feelings, and memories I've been holding onto are

_____

Holding onto all this has hurt our relationship in the following ways

_____

I want to build a better relationship, based on the following value

_____

Use the separate Values and Priorities worksheets on page 183 to set your blueprint for moving forward.

STEP 2: Write your own "letting go" commitment

My commitment is to

_____

STEP 3: Choose a special place to read your answers to each other.

As the person reads their commitment, it is received in silence and with loving, full attention. This is no time for "yes but's" or "I already do that" comments. This is truly listening—heart and soul listening.

STEP 4: Celebrate starting over.

Do something, right away, not next week, or when we have time. Do it NOW! Hug. Burn the letters. Go for a walk. Watch a funny movie. Go for a special dinner.

Appreciating Your Partner

Fill in this form each day. Notice (at least) three things you appreciate about your partner. They don't have to be big things—they might even be the way he smiles or the sound of her laughter.

3 Things I noticed today that I appreciate about my partner	3 Ways my partner contributed to my life today	3 Things my partner said or did today that represent their best strengths and qualities
1.	1.	1.
2.	2.	2.
3.	3.	3.

[from *ACT With Love*, Russ Harris]

Your Parents' Life Values

My Father's Life Values are:

_____

_____

_____

(e.g., hard work, pride, family, ethnic heritage, and so on.)

My Mother's Life Values are:

_____

_____

_____

(e.g., family, education, keeping face, helping people, and so on.)

Take a thoughtful look at what you believe their values are, put yourself in their head, and imagine how they are feeling around the issues of losing their freedom, their vitality, and their choices. It will help you to be kinder and more understanding when you get push-back—because you will.

In-Law Appreciation Chart

On days that may be more trying than others, you might want to remind yourself of the good times, the blessings you've been given by your partner's family:

3 things I appreciate about my mother/father/ sister/brother-in-law	3 ways my in-laws contribute positively to my life	3 things my in-laws said or did today/this week that represent their best qualities and strengths
1.	1.	1.
2.	2.	2.
3.	3.	3.

The Six Human Needs

Choose your top two:

- Certainty
- Variety
- Significance
- Love and Connection
- Growth
- Contribution

How do your needs serve you currently in your view of your world?

Look at your old story and move into your new story
(*"We can do this together"*).

Use blame to move forward—bad blame and good blame
(*"We can do this together"*).

The Three Buttons

Here are the three buttons that most people have:

- I'm not good enough (as a parent, a partner, a person).
- I'm stupid.
- I'm irrelevant (my thoughts and feelings don't matter).

Tell yourself, *Not anymore!* You now know what to do:

- Look at it;
- Acknowledge it; and
- Let it go.

Values And Priorities: Setting Goals

Values	Priorities
Family	Peaceful interaction with kids
Healthy living	Activities with kids
Respect	Careful, considered communicating
Kindness	Don't speak badly about ex
Friends	Laugh and have fun with friends
Good work ethic	Take courses for a career

If you partner these Priorities alongside your Values, you can then set goals—how you're going to manage the next six months with your head held high.

Who Are You?

Let's find out. Answer these simple questions (that are not so simple), and you'll have more idea of who and how you are. That way you'll know more about what you're looking for in a date and a mate.

WHO am I?

(Sample answer: I am male/female [age]. I am a daughter, mother, son, father, friend, and I have a career/job as a _____ , which I find satisfying, etc., etc., etc.)

Who AM I?

(Sample answer: My spirit is connected through my awareness of [religion, spirituality, meditation, etc., etc.] my highest self, and through this I know that I AM.)

Who am I?

(Sample answer: I am joy in the springtime, playing hockey with the guys, celebrating my part in family, surrounding myself with music and nature, etc.)

Changes In Friendship Values And Priorities

Check in and see how our Values and Priorities may have changed over the past 20 years or more.

My key Life Values today are:

1. _____

2. _____

3. _____

4. _____

5. _____

My key Priorities are:

1. _____

2. _____

3. _____

4. _____

5. _____

Current Limitations in my life are: *(e.g. time, no car, etc.)*

1. _____

2. _____

3. _____

4. _____

5. _____

When I was younger I wanted my friend to:

- Be easily available (at school or next door, etc.)
- Be fun to laugh and giggle with
- Play "pretend" with me
- Talk about our dreams
- And... (you add to the list here)

Now I want a friend to be:

- kind
- a good listener
- available to do things with
- fun
- (you add to the list here)

... and notice the difference.

Life Values Changes Chart

List and look at your Life Values, and see how you can apply them to this relationship. For example, if one of your Values is Kindness, then use it, knowing that how you change will change the relationship and the energy around it. Once you change the energy, everything changes.

Life Values:

1. _____

2. _____

3. _____

4. _____

5. _____

How I might use these to change
the relationship with (*name*)_____

1. _____

2. _____

3. _____

4. _____

5. _____

When this happens _____

and I feel _____

I will take a deep breath, remembering my values and commitment to harmony, peace, and empowerment, and I will respond this way:

_____

Knowing how you respond to any situation is the first step to change. We can't change anything until we know what we're changing. And change takes time, in addition to awareness. How we respond to others is a pattern, a habit, stemming from old responses. Habits and patterns take time to change, but awareness *comes first* and is a must.

Here goes! Ask yourself:

- How am I inappropriately feeling and acting in this situation?
- What's going through my head, and what am I feeling in my body to respond this way? Irritable? Self-righteous? Fearful? Resentful?
- About myself?
- About the others?
- About the situation?

What can I realistically substitute for my awful-izing, should-ing, and rationalizing? How about:

- I want...
- I'd like...
- I'd prefer...
- It would be better if...
- What feelings would result if...?
- It's unfortunate...
- I'm disappointed ...
- I'm seriously concerned...
- I regret...
- I'm committed to...

SWOT

(Strengths, Weaknesses, Opportunities, Threats)

Here are some suggested categories for analysis:

Strengths

- Education
- Work ethic
- Transferable skills
- Personality attributes
- Work experience
- Character
- Training ability
- Community profile, etc.
- Add others here

Weaknesses

- Weak planning or execution abilities
- Lack of focus
- Low energy
- Little relevant experience
- Weak detail or big picture focus
- Lack of ability to prioritize
- Lack of time management skills
- Add others

Opportunities

- Self-growth
- Networking
- Building bottom line from X to XX in first, second, and third year
- New markets
- Training programs

- Inter-company exchange program
- Add others

Threats

- Growth of competition
- Management changes
- Slow business
- Office disruptions
- Add others

One Last Exercise – What Needs Work?

What Is Working for Me Currently, and What Still Needs Attention?

I am grateful that these relationships are now working well for me	These pieces of my life need attention
1.	1.
2.	2.
3.	3.
4.	4.
5.	5.
6.	6.

Let your "pieces" that need attention become your goals for the forthcoming months.

> *Mind:* What will you achieve by when?
> *Body:* What will you have done by when?
> *Spirituality:* How will you be behaving by when?
> *Relationship hiccups:* What will be different by when?

References

INTRODUCTION

Ruthellen Josselson, Jason Aronson. *Playing Pygmalion: How People Create One Another*. Jason Aronson: New York, NY. 2007, Ch. 7 ("Pygmalion and Galatea").

CHAPTER 1

Julia B. Colwell *The Relationship Skills Workbook*. Ph.D. Sounds True: Boulder, CO. 2014, p. 106.

—— *The Relationship Skills Workbook.*, Ph.D. Sounds True: Boulder, CO. 2014, p.161.

CHAPTER 2

Phillip C. McGraw. *Life Strategies: Doing What Works, Doing What Matters*. Ph.D. Hyperion: New York, NY. 1999, p. 67–68.

CHAPTER 4

Lisa A. Philips. "It's Over" in *Psychology Today*. May/June 2015, p.78 ff.

Russ Harris. *ACT With Love*. *www.act-with-love.com*. 2009. Ch. 1.

Ruthellen Josselson, Jason Aronson. *Playing Pygmalion: How People Create One Another*. Jason Aronson: New York, NY. 2007, Ch. 7 ("Pygmalion and Galatea").

CHAPTER 5

Albert Ellis, Ph.D. & Arthur Lange, Ed.D. *How to Keep People From Pushing Your Buttons*. A Birch Lane Press Book, Carol Publishing Group: New York, NY. 1994, p. 70–71.

Julia B. Colwell. *The Relationship Skills Workbook*. Ph.D. Sounds True: Boulder, CO. 2014. p. 139.

CHAPTER 6

Ruthellen Josselson, Jason Aronson. *Playing Pygmalion: How People Create One Another*. Jason Aronson: New York, NY. 2007, Ch. 7 ("Pygmalion and Galatea").

Ken Blanchard. *The One Minute Manager*. *http://modernservantleader.com/servant-leadership/do-you-have-a-*seagull-manager.

CHAPTER 7

Elisabeth Graham. "The Other Woman" in *Marriage Partnership Magazine*.

Romie Hurley. *Focus on the Family's Complete Guide to the First Five Years of Marriage*. Tyndale, 2006.

Ingrid Lawrenz. "In-Law Tug-of-War" in *Marriage Partnership Magazine*.

CHAPTER 8

Albert Ellis, Ph.D. & Arthur Lange, Ed.D. *How to Keep People From Pushing Your Buttons*. A Birch Lane Press Book, Carol Publishing Group: New York, NY. 1994, P. 70.

Lisa A. Philips. "It's Over" in *Psychology Today*. May/June 2015, p.78.

CHAPTER 12

Phillip C. McGraw, Ph.D. *Life Strategies: Doing What Works, Doing What Matters*. Hyperion: New York, NY. 1999, pp. 255–262.

CHAPTER 13

Rick Pitino with Bill Reynolds. *Success is a Choice: Ten steps to Overachieving in Business and Life*. Broadway Books: New York, NY. 1997. p. 36.

FINDHORN PRESS

Life-Changing Books

Consult our catalogue online
(with secure order facility) on
www.findhornpress.com

For information on the Findhorn Foundation:
www.findhorn.org